Val Sines

Martha Morton

Alpha Editions

This edition published in 2024

ISBN : 9789362921383

Design and Setting By
Alpha Editions
www.alphaedis.com
Email - info@alphaedis.com

Contents

BOOK I

"The lives of men and women are pictures thrown upon the screen of Time.

The Past—its misty perspective, its legendary charm; Truth veiled in Fiction."

BOOK I

1

ABOUT twenty-five years ago, Pedro Gonzola bought that handsome brown stone residence at the corner of Twelfth Street and Fifth Avenue, and presented it to his bride on their wedding day. As the name implied, they were of Spanish origin, and known as devout Catholics, supporting the Church spiritually and materially.

Shortly before Julie was born, her father died suddenly, stricken down with heart failure. The young widow was stunned by the loss of her handsome adoring husband; her uncontrollable grief nearly cost her the life of her coming child, who suffered from her mother's anguish—at least that's what the good Dr. McClaren said.

After her great misfortune Mrs. Gonzola gave up the world and devoted herself to her religion and the care of her little daughter. Julie was sent to the Convent of the Sacred Heart in Seventeenth Street. The Sisters educated her under the personal supervision of her mother; their reports were satisfactory; the child was docile and receptive, but inclined to emotional exaggeration; she would remain in the chapel long after the other children had left, and once they found her prostrate before the Virgin in a state of ecstatic self-oblivion, which ended in a fit of hysteria. There was no cause for worry, as otherwise she was "full of life" and a general favorite. Mrs. Gonzola tried conscientiously to impress her daughter with the dignity of her wealth, social position, and family distinction; but as the girl grew into a woman, there was an ever-present irritating sense of failure.

Julie Gonzola at sixteen, with her brilliant exotic beauty, was a mystery to her friends, her mother, herself. She was acutely conscious of strange emotions, which she instinctively concealed; hers was a nature of unexpected impulses, tragic possibilities, baffling secrets. She came of an old stock on her father's side, and on her mother's she could look down a long corridor, where she saw shadowy forms, which frightened her. She was different from her girl friend, who was care-free, bubbling, sparkling, dashing along like a brook which overflows its bounds out of sheer rapture.

Maud Ailsworth lived down the street. There were no complications in *her* life. She ruled her mother, who was an invalid, and physically her inferior. Maud romped all day long in the street with the boys. Mrs. Gonzola never allowed Julie to do that; she was very indulgent in her way, denying the girl nothing—but freedom. Julie was outwardly submissive; she was sorry for her mother, who sat alone in her room crying, silent iron tears of impotent despair.

There were two boys in the street whom Maud liked; as she grew older she determined to marry one of them, but she found to her great disappointment they were both hot after Julie. Floyd Garrison, a pretty boy of an old American family, was very well brought up; Martin Steele was a mongrel, a brute, a ruffian, but there was something very likable about him. Maud looked on, watched them wrestling for the privilege of carrying Julie's books when she came from school, with her maid. There were fist fights for her as children, rivalry as youths, and bitterness as men. But Maud wasn't discouraged; Julie couldn't marry both of them; there would be always one left for her. Then she had Tom Dillon in reserve; he was common, but she owned him; he was her slave.

Julie was afraid of Martin Steele; he had bad manners and a violent temper. He was always mussing up her hair, and winding her curls around his fingers. Floyd was too polite to do that. There was a party at Maud Ailsworth's; Tom Dillon, that mischievous imp, put out the lights. The boy next to Julie kissed her, pressing her to him with terrible force; it was Martin. After that, he kissed her whenever he found her alone, and he managed it often. She liked his hot unboyish kisses.

2

The Garrisons had lived four generations in a little wooden house in East Twelfth Street, "a very pretty shanty" Martin called it, set back, with a garden, and a wooden fence to protect the lawn and flowers from passing vandals.

A portrait of the ancestor who founded the family fortune hangs today in our Museum. "Yan Geritsen, baker," endowed with business sagacity, bought land under water in New Amsterdam for "thirty cents," left it to his son, with orders not to sell. Succeeding generations drained and developed it. The name smelt of newly baked bread; it gradually evolved itself into Garrison. They were one of the fast disappearing families, who remained as they began—modest and thankful. They brought up their son with a sense of responsibility, as trustee for the coming son. There were no girls as far back as could be remembered; each family branch had one son. Floyd's father, "Jimmy" Garrison, married a school marm. He became acquainted with her in Boston. She was very poor, but descended from *the* Aldens. Prudence Alden was a pale silent girl with a hidden fountain of irrepressible love in all its rare purity. Young Garrison's friends couldn't see what *he* saw in her.

Garrison had never been in business; he disliked the everlasting talk about money which was rapidly becoming God under the title of the "Almighty" dollar. He had many acquaintances and one faithful friend, Colonel Garland, a Southern gentleman, who had made a reputation "up North" as a corporation lawyer, when trusts were springing up over night like toadstools. The Colonel retained his sombrero, his soft accent, his passionate devotion to a few friends, and many women. When Jimmy Garrison put the administration of his estate into Colonel Garland's hands, it was intact, just as his father had left it.

"Let us pull down those old hulks and build up warehouses," said the Colonel. Garrison refused to consider that.

"The estate was not bought yesterday, for speculation. It has always brought us enough to live on modestly, and something over; if I get four per cent., I'm well satisfied."

In time, modern buildings were erected on both sides of the Garrison "hulks," which, although kept clean and in repair, had to be rented below the market value. Conservative policy has its good side; many went under in the frenzy of over-building. In such a young country the cult of silence, material rest, creative thought were as yet unknown; the man who did not create capital was considered an idler; Garrison continued to the end of his peaceful, worryless life, a gentleman.

The first realization of pain was the sudden death of his beloved Prudence; he had to live for his boy and looked about, seeking a sustaining force.

He rigged up a workshop in the top of his house, and took to modeling figures, which were very well done—every-day people he had known, the little Italian shoe boy, the newspaper woman, his friends, idealized of course, his wife in every mood, his boy. He was particularly successful with a smiling old Irishman, a pipe in his mouth, a hod on his shoulder, standing at the foot of a ladder looking upward. He called that figure "the Ancestor," which title was a secret source of amusement to him, although he was too good-natured to say *whose* ancestor.

When asked the inevitable question,

"What business are you in, Mr. Garrison?"

Garrison would answer gravely,

"I muddle in clay."

3

The Steeles lived next door to the Garrisons in an ugly high-stoop, four-story brick mansion, which threw a dark shadow on one side of the little garden, necessitating Garrison to move his flower-beds away.

Martin was five years older than Floyd and twenty years more experienced. He loved Floyd in his way, but love was not an element of his nature. Floyd looked up to him, as a little boy would to an elder one who condescended to be his friend; he was sorry for Martin because Mrs. Steele was only his stepmother, that was what was wrong with him—he never had a "real" mother. Mrs. Steele was born Dolly Winthrop of Boston; she was very tall, very thin, very straight, with small transparent ears lying flat against her head. The only large thing about her was her flow of language—that was tremendous. Mrs. Steele's "family tree" reposed on the parlor table in a red velvet album—"reposed" is a very inappropriate word, for she never gave the poor thing any rest. She was constantly turning over its pages, adding, multiplying, never subtracting, until it fell quite to pieces, but she convinced the old New Yorkers of her right to be one of them.

The "exclusives" of Massachusetts never forgave Dolly Winthrop's marriage with "that Steele man" who was fat, florid, wordless, and a widower with a child. There were still spots in the Union where pedigree and culture were of more value than "money"; but Dolly Winthrop had made her calculation and it turned out a good bargain. Her husband and his father devoted all their time to business; they accumulated great wealth, and were not perceptible in her richly woven society tapestry. There was one she couldn't wipe out—that terrible boy Martin. She tried honestly to make something of him, but he was not to be moulded. She took him to her summer home in Nantucket. The Winthrop Homestead had ship-lamps, a model of the *Mayflower*, clocks that struck "bells"—numbered hours were disdained; there were also stuffed seagulls which Martin set up as skittles, and a tottering old sailor who took care of the garden and gave the necessary atmosphere. Aunt Priscilla, Mrs. Steele's maiden sister, lived there all the year. In Nantucket, Martin's capacity of hatred found fertile soil for expansion; he hated the ocean; its unceasing roar fretted him; he thought of a big sea monster in chains, writhing, howling, foaming at the mouth. He hated Aunt Priscilla, who was Calvinist, Puritan, Patriot, anti-everything else. She took unusual pains to enlighten the "little savage" about the distinguished pedigree of his stepmother's family. One day she read to him for three hours, in her correct English "twang," the history of those good old Colonial times, when her direct ancestor was a Judge in Salem. The boy's eyes took on a glitter which meant mischief.

"I'd like to be a Judge in them times."

"You mean, you'd like to *have* been a Judge in *those* times," corrected Aunt Priscilla.

"Have been," mumbled the boy.

Aunt Priscilla was delighted; at last she had awakened the pride of ancestry in that little soul.

"Now tell me, dear, what would you *have done* if you *had been* a Judge in Salem."

"I'd burn you."

4

One day Floyd found out there was a mystery on the top floor of the Steele house; it was Martin's fourteenth birthday. He invited Floyd to ice-cream and cake. "Julie Gonzola was coming." There was plenty to eat, but Floyd lost his appetite looking at little Julie sitting up on a high chair with all the best things piled before her. She let Martin pile them, but she didn't touch them—she couldn't, in a strange house.

Toward evening the maid came to take her home. The two boys stood at the window as she went past enveloped in white furs, her little feet stepping out firmly, her head erect.

Martin's eyes snapped.

"I'm going to marry Julie."

"Not if I know it."

Martin turned and swept the boy with a cold disdain terrible in one so young. It hurt Floyd; he remembered that look, years after. He said nothing, but turned to go.

Martin stopped him.

"Stay with me; I'm lonesome."

There was a touch of pathos in his voice.

"Come, I'll show you some family relics."

He led the way to the garret, four stories high; it was filled with old furniture, spinning wheels, oil paintings—some wretchedly bad, others fairly good, all with heavy gold frames; every piece was ticketed with a name and date, in the different generations of the family.

Then Martin became confidential.

"I'll tell you something, but don't mention it to my mother. These things are all fakes; she haunts the auction sales, she's a good judge—she knows what fits in, she's got a whole lot more in storage. We're going to move away from here."

Floyd got a chill.

"What! You were born here! You will never leave your home?"

Martin's mocking laugh rang out.

"Oh, you're too sentimental. She's not going to sell the house; that wouldn't look well. She's going to fill it with our 'family' antiques, and donate it to the city as an 'Art Museum.'"

Floyd was struck silent as usual by Martin's terrible lack of heart.

"What's that?"

"What?"

"Somebody singing."

Martin looked troubled.

"Nonsense, there's nobody up here. Let's go down."

He drew Floyd into the hall; there was a door opposite.

It *was* somebody singing—a man's voice, broken, harsh, rising, and falling in a strange inflection.

Martin, with a look of fear mingled with shame, tried to draw Floyd downstairs. A heavy fist on the door pushed it open. A man of gigantic stature rushed out. At first glance, Floyd saw only a pair of wonderful mocking eyes—Martin's eyes; there was a strange light in them. The man was mad. Martin sprang at him, tried to push him back into the room. He was too strong for the boy. Then Martin coaxed him. Was that Martin's voice, so loving, so sweet? He spoke in a foreign tongue, strange to Floyd. The old man looked curiously at Floyd, then said "Grutsie" and bowed respectfully. He learnt afterwards "Grutsie" was Swiss dialect for "I greet you."

The man had huge hands, knotty, sun-dried; the open flannel shirt revealed a chest covered with thick hair. He had an enormous head, and a thick white mane falling over his eyes. He wore corduroy trousers to the knees and a pair of high deerskin boots with heavy nails in the soles. He paced unceasingly. The floor was covered with indentures. Martin shut the door carefully, took down a harness with bells which hung on the wall, threw it over the old man's head, cracking a heavy whip, yelling at the top of his voice, lashing him with sharp quick blows. The old man growled like a beaten beast; the whip hurt him; the young devil was strong; in the sensual intoxication of brute force, they forgot the horrified boy looking on.

The door was flung open. Mrs. Steele stood there, deathly pale.

"Stop that noise, you'll rouse the neighbors; how dare you bring Floyd up here?" She grasped Martin's hand, pushing him toward the door.

The old man slunk into a corner; he was evidently afraid of her.

"Let me go!" roared Martin.

"I won't. You'll be punished for this." Then a struggle followed; Floyd never forgot it. She held him with her small strong hands; he bit them. She struck him across the mouth; he kicked her. She cried out with pain, but she held him fast. Floyd, with a terrified cry, rushed down the stairs and out of the house.

5

Mr. Garrison was working at his clay figures, thinking how much Floyd was growing like his mother; he had her sensitive, ideal nature. The boy's love for Julie might be a great blessing; it might be the contrary.... He would like to live long enough to see that beautiful little girl a woman.

Floyd broke into the room, sobbing out what he had seen. Mr. Garrison quieted him, and told him the story of the Steele family, as he had it from his friend, Colonel Garland.

The old man in the garret was Martin's grandfather, a Swiss peasant, who had come to America in the steerage, with his boy, a child of four. He obtained a position as waiter in a downtown cafe, and the boy grew up in the streets. In ten years the father was head waiter in a Fifth Avenue hotel, frequented by Wall Street men. He never spoke more than a waiter's English. His boy came out of school with a correct knowledge of grammar, but was silent, uncouth, unfriendly. Waiting for his father one night, in the kitchen of the hotel, he noticed one of the dishwashers, a very young blonde girl, crying bitterly. He questioned her; she told him she was Swiss, like himself, that she had been in America a short time, and was very unhappy. He comforted her. When it became no longer possible to conceal her condition, he married her; this was a bitter blow to the old waiter, who had, in those twenty years of deprivation, saved one hundred thousand dollars, and wanted to make a gentleman out of his son. Fate favored him. The girl died giving birth to a boy. The doctors could not understand the case; she was a very strong, healthy peasant; but Martin in a burst of anguish insisted she had died of homesickness.

Mr. Garrison explained to Floyd the word "nostalgia," originating with the Swiss, which meant their longing for their native soil when absent; the pain is intolerable, ending often in death. Floyd was very sorry for the poor peasant mother.

"Then what happened?"

"The old man started in the hotel supply business; he rented one of my shanties on the river front. The firm is still there. I used to see old Steele walking up and down before that sign on the door. 'Martin Steele and Son.' I could never make friends with young Steele; he was sullen, wordless, and seemed to be out of his element. Then they bought the house next door and lived there a solitary life. Your mother was sorry for lonely little Martin, and had him often in here to play with you. When Dolly Winthrop came from Boston to visit us, we saw she had her eye on the rich widower."

"And she got him," said Floyd.

"Yes, unfortunately for him."

"And what happened then, father?"

"She dominated those poor men with her culture, shamed them with her pedigree, crushed them with her contempt. The old man fell into bad habits, drank to excess. His mind failed; people spoke of an illiterate grandfather in the house, but visitors never saw him.".....

After that episode in the garret, Mrs. Steele's patience with the boy gave out. She insisted on sending him to a strict military school. He'd come home in the summertime when she was in Nantucket, and prowl about the city during the long evenings. In Twelfth Street, seemingly deserted, he'd run up and down stoops, pulling bells; then the "spring rollers" would fly up, and he'd count the genteel poor who were sweltering in New York; when he grew too old for such pranks, he would spend his evenings in the garret watching his father and grandfather playing a strange game of cards called "Tarac" and listening to their jargon. He learnt the game and the jargon, with great rapidity.

His father, who was always afraid of troubling his wife, died suddenly at his desk; then the old man's mind bolted.

Mrs. Steele in a burst of confidence said one day to Mr. Garrison:

"It may be very wicked of me, but I pray to God not to let him live long." Her prayer was answered; unrighteous prayers usually are. After that, Mrs. Steele closed the house and went to live in Boston; later she sent Martin to Harvard. Floyd wrote him several times, but his letters were not answered; it was many years before the two boys met again.

6

Floyd didn't go to college—his father couldn't spare him, but he gave him a good classical education, under the best professors. Mr. Garrison wasn't training his son for business; he wanted him to be a man of culture. They took long walks into the country, with Emerson, Hawthorne, Longfellow for companions. Thoreau was revolutionary, a disjointed mind. The historical novels then in vogue were read and reread, also foreign literature. Realism, Nihilism, and all the other isms were looked into and studied as the result of "unhealthy" European conditions. Mr. Garrison moulded his son in good clay.

Sunday was the happiest day in the week for Floyd. He would slip out of the little Dutch Reform church around the corner, restless when the pastor strung out his sermon fearing he should miss Julie, who went to the Cathedral. Lately, he was fortunate to find her there without her mother.

Good Friday,—the Cathedral draped in black. The sorrow-laden music, the odor of incense gave him a sensuous feeling of emotion. Julie came down the aisle, her prayer book pressed against her heart, her eyes seeking things beyond this world. It seemed to the impressionable youth a desecration to "bring her back."

He looked at the sad faces and bowed heads.

"It's wonderful after so many centuries, this sense of personal loss in the people; life would be unbearable without the Easter joy, the lilies, the Resurrection."

His words sounded poetical to him as he spoke; he was very young. Julie smiled; she seemed less divine out in the sunlight.

"I don't feel that way, but Mother is ill and insists on my going; an empty pew doesn't look well."

Floyd was shocked. He had read in the "great" writers those traditional truisms we repeat mechanically. "The woman's emotional nature endows her with the gift of Faith; she has held aloft the Banner of Religion in the great struggle against skepticism."

They walked down Fifth Avenue. There was an expression he had never seen in Julie's calm face, an indefinable something, as if she had pulled down a veil over her eyes. Before her house, she didn't give him her hand as usual. She was looking expectantly at the upper windows; he followed her gaze. She waved her hand, smilingly; there was a face looking out; the light made it transparent like yellow wax. In a moment it was gone.

"Who was that?"

"My grandfather."

"Why haven't I seen him before?"

"He doesn't come downstairs."

"Is he ill?"

"No. I've wanted to tell you for some time, but Mother said it was nobody's business."

Floyd was hurt.

"Anything that concerns you is of vital interest to me. You know that, don't you, Julie?"

"Yes, I know it."

She braced her shoulders, looking him straight in the face; she was very proud. He liked that; most girls held themselves too cheaply.

"My grandfather doesn't come down because he disapproves of the way we live. He says we have sold our souls."

"I don't understand you."

"We are Jews. You needn't come here again." She went quickly up the steps and entered the house without looking back.

Floyd walked down the street towards his house. He was terribly excited; socially, he had never known any Jews. He had seen some dark fellows who were wonders at mathematics and chess; boys of their creed were limited in numbers in the colleges, kept out of social clubs, but somehow they managed to filter through everywhere. What did it mean? How could the Gonzolas be Jews? They were Catholics.

A young man came towards him, of striking appearance, with a touch of something about him not American. He put out his hand laughingly to Floyd. It was Martin.

"You've done with me?"

"You deserve it. Why didn't you answer my letters?"

"Oh! I had no time; they kept my nose to the grindstone. I walked off with the prizes just to spite Aunt Priscilla. Mother is very proud of me; she calls me 'my son' now." There was the old mocking glitter in his eye; he had not changed.

"Don't be angry with me." He took Floyd's arm. Martin could be very winning when he wanted to. "You've grown into a fine, handsome fellow, with the unmistakable brand of the aristocrat; strong with the women, eh?"

"I don't know."

"As gone as ever on Julie?"

"More than ever."

Then Floyd shot out a question.

"Do you know the history of the Gonzolas?"

Martin's answer came back as quickly.

"Yes, they are baptized Jews."

A red streak flushed Floyd's forehead.

"Tell me about them."

Martin leaned against the gate, revelling in Floyd's agitation.

"The Gonzolas go back to the time when the Church in Spain commenced war on the Jews; thousands of them were baptized, but they still practiced their religion in secret. Romantic, isn't it?"

"No; terrible."

"Many of the Catholic Gonzolas became Bishops, Cardinals, and high state officials on account of their wealth and culture, but others, true to their Faith, fled to Amsterdam, where they founded the great banking house which spread its branches all over Europe. Julie's grandfather was a handsome, dashing fellow. He married in the family—they all do—but he had an affair with an Austrian actress which lasted for years. Their son was brought up in the religion of his mother who became pious with age and as expiation, dedicated him to the Church. She died before he was ordained, and Gonzola, naturally opposed, easily persuaded the boy against it—and sent him to America where he took the family name. The bank he founded here was successful; he became very rich. This bastard was Julie's father."

"But they are Catholics, not Jews," insisted Floyd.

"That's the joke of it," laughed Martin. "An ironic witticism, an impish trick of Fate. Pedro came with letters from his father, to an old friend, Joseph Abravanel, an orthodox Jew, a fanatic, of Spanish origin with infernal pride of race. He boasts his ancestors provided money to help Columbus fit out his ship. Pedro fell desperately in love with Ruth Abravanel; those Spanish Jewesses are handsome, but most of them are old maids, because they won't marry the Germans whom they look down upon."

"That old man I saw today at the window?"

"Is Joseph Abravanel, Mrs. Gonzola's father."

"But how did you know all this?"

"I've heard it scores of times from Julie. The crossing of the races interests me; I've got my own ideas about that. I'm waiting to see how it comes out."

"It's shocking for people to change their religion."

Martin laughed a bit too loud, Floyd thought.

"What's the difference? Who believes in it anyhow; do you?"

Floyd evaded a direct answer.

"We practice many things out of respect for our parents and our social position." He was undeniably well brought up.

"There's one thing I like about Julie," said Martin. "In spite of everything, she remains a true daughter of her race. I like in her the sensuousness of the Oriental; oh, I don't mean sexness—that may also be there latent; I hope it is. I see in her the Shulamite maiden who gets up from her couch at night and goes to seek her lover."

"What do you know about Julie? You've been away so long."

"I've been a week in New York."

Floyd was angry, injured. "Perhaps you've been writing to her all this time."

"Perhaps I have."

"I suppose she was very glad to see you."

"I don't know. I was mad to see her. I couldn't wait; I went straight there."

There was a look of passion in Martin's face. Floyd hated him. He turned and entered the gate. Martin was at his elbow.

"I'm coming in to see your father."

At dinner Martin kept up a fire of witty criticisms. Floyd was silent, preoccupied.

"Your house has been shut up for some time. Where is your mother?"

"In Nantucket. She loves the shores where her ancestors landed, in sailing vessels."

"Your mother's pride of nationality is quite natural; I also feel it."

"You don't parade it. My mother makes capital out of it."

"But," insisted Mr. Garrison, "you are an American; you were born here; you know no other home. English is your mother tongue."

"Yes, but race is stronger than language. My people were Swiss peasants. I may look and speak like a gentleman, but sometimes the lout in me is hard to suppress."

There was a silence. Mr. Garrison changed the subject.

"Are you going into your father's business?"

"No—I'd smash it with my mad notions." Then he flashed a bright look. "I've been daubing in oil; it's the only thing that interests me. I shall go to Paris to study, if I live."

Mr. Garrison was all animation. "That's very good news. You will live; you're young, strong."

"Who knows—America is going into the wholesale slaughter business. She needs butchers."

"You mean—"

"I think we'll be pushed into the War."

Floyd was all attention. He spoke with a thrill in his voice.

"If it comes, we Americans will not be wanting in patriotism."

Martin didn't seem to feel the insinuation.

"Patriotism, bah! Who cares? We'll have to go; if we don't, they'll shoot us."

Mr. Garrison was sitting with his head in his hands. Floyd arose and went to him. He had been failing for some time, complained of dizziness. Dr. McClaren couldn't discover any organic trouble. Floyd, who watched every change of expression, saw him grow pale.

"Father—you don't feel well."

"Oh yes!—but I think I'll go and rest awhile."

He rose from the chair, staggered; Martin caught him, carried him up, and laid him on the bed.

Floyd bent over his father, frantically begging him to speak. The stricken man raised his hand in a mute blessing, then closed his eyes.

To Floyd, the next few weeks were chaotic; time, space, light, darkness lost all meaning. Martin never left him during those black days; always there in the sleepless horror of the night, to read to him, to go out and pace the streets with him, when the walls became insupportable. He would have gone under without Martin.

The funeral over, the will read by Colonel Garland, the sole executor, the few distant relatives from far and near come and gone, Floyd took up again the routine of life. Mr. Garrison had left everything to his son, whom he hoped would marry young and be happy in the old home, leaving it to *his* son after him. The Garrisons had always lived well, in a modest way, befitting their position. He was sure Floyd would keep up the family tradition. He left money to many philanthropic institutions and to his club where he and his father before him had spent many pleasant hours and where he hoped his boy would sit many years after him.

Colonel Garland, commenting on the will to Martin, said:

"A sane, righteous testament. He was a good man...."

7

In the months that followed, Floyd saw little of Julie. She called several times with her mother, who was very sweet and amiable.

"I hope when you feel more like seeing people you'll come to us often," said Mrs. Gonzola.

Floyd looked at Julie, who smiled at him, and returned the pressure of his hand. Martin was a great deal at the Gonzolas', but he didn't mention that to Floyd. One Sunday afternoon Mrs. Gonzola came into the parlor, Martin was sitting very close to Julie, reading in rich passionate tones a love poem by Oscar Wilde; Julie started up and Martin left, but all that day she couldn't meet her mother's clairvoyant eyes.

"I don't like him, Julie. He's no class. He was an unmannerly boy and he's a dangerous man. I've told James to say you're out, the next time he calls. If you meet him accidentally, avoid him."

"Yes, Mother," said Julie. After that she saw him often with the assistance of a sympathetic French teacher, whose room was post-office and rendezvous for the lovers.

Martin gave Julie glimpses of "life." He took her to all kinds of strange places—a chop suey restaurant, with its unpalatable dishes, soft lights, and insidious Chinamen; a dancing cafe which at that time was not supposed to be a place for young ladies—but best of all was Hippolyte.

Hippolyte's Parlor flaunted on Fifth Avenue. It had a magnificent plate glass show window, fitted with Circassian walnut, in which was one red feather fan on a cushion of Nile green velvet, one jeweled comb, and a Pierrot costumed in black silk with a large white ruff, his face wonderful in its languid perversity. Up the side street there was a private door which opened halfway to let in ladies heavily veiled. Julie's ambition was to see what was behind that fascinating door; today it is no longer a mystery. In the Middle Ages, Hippolyte would have been a miracle man summoned to a fair Venetian to deepen the red of her hair, the rose in her cheeks, the marvel of her eyes— selling for a purse of gold, charms to rob a rival of a coveted lover. Times have not changed, nor people; only appearances.

Martin took Julie into the shop one day and introduced her to Hippolyte, who pronounced her "ravissante"; thereupon Martin bought a costly box of perfume. Julie was afraid to take it home.

"I'll settle that," laughed Martin, and poured it over her, then they ran around the reservoir to get rid of the odor. Mrs. Gonzola noticed it, but said nothing.

Julie was standing at the window waiting for her mother. Her gloved hands impatiently agitating the curtains.

"Mother, the car is here. I shall be late for my music lesson."

The voice answering from upstairs was nervous, trembling. "It's impossible for me to go with you today; I'm not well."

A flash illumined Julie's face, but her voice was under perfect control. "I'm sorry."

From the upper window, her mother watched her, music-roll in hand, stepping into the car. Mrs. Gonzola realized more and more acutely that her lovely child was developing into a beautiful woman; there was no feeling of joyful pride. Horrible, agonizing fear stopped the current of her blood.

Julie, alone in the car, drew a long breath. The pink of her lips turned red, the color slowly overflowing into her cheeks. She pulled the cord, asked the chauffeur in her soft, sensuous voice to stop at the nearest drug store; there she telephoned, then drove to the house of her professor. She was a gifted pianiste; she played with a sure, velvety touch, surmounting with ease all technical difficulties. The professor went into ecstasies about the beautiful child-woman with "Eternal Love in her fingers."

The car turned into the Park. Martin was walking up and down by the little lake. He hated to wait. She never kept an appointment; if she didn't come today he was through. His heart leaped when he saw her. The girl had a terrible power over him. She said smilingly:

"We'll go across town and up Riverside Drive for an hour. Then I'll drop you at the club."

They sped along in the car. He pulled down the shades, drew off her gloves, tearing the buttons in his haste, crushed her two hands in his moist hot ones, spoke quickly, panting with excitement:

"I've thought it all out. I'm going to your mother tonight."

"No! No!" gasped Julie. "Write to her first."

"I have written to her, as politely as I knew how. I told her I loved you and wanted you to be my wife."

He read the answer, his voice shaking with anger and wounded pride:

I have no words to reply to your impertinent letter. Julie will not marry until she is of age. You are not the man I consider worthy of her. You take it for granted that she is willing. I know her better. She will not consent. I warn you not to molest her with further attentions, and consider the matter closed.

She crouched in the corner, speechless.

"She will blame me. She will say I encouraged you."

"You did, didn't you?"

"Yes, but marriage! I'm too young yet."

He pressed her to him with a force that left her helpless. He would show her haughty mother who was the master. With his face pressed against hers, he talked, expostulated, begged, threatened to kill himself, kissing her again and again, until she gave in. She would do anything, everything he asked of her, but he must give her twenty-four hours to win over her mother.

"If you fail?"

"Then, I will go with you."

"You promise."

"Yes."

"Julie! Your mother will influence you against me!"

"No one can do that."

"You are mine; I will not give you up." He swore an oath, which made her shudder. With a quiver of terrible joy, she put her arms around his neck. Her lips sought his.

8

Every afternoon, Floyd Garrison occupied a deep chair in the window of his club on upper Fifth Avenue—a privilege inherited by the law of precedence, from his father and grandfather. His great-grandfather was one of the founders of the original club-house which was downtown—an old building with raftered ceilings, wooden models of ships, and a portrait of Peter with the game leg.

In time the "youngsters" of 1850 moved uptown, refurnished in plush, and became very exclusive. They kept people out for lack of pedigree, or difference of religious conviction.

A young scion of the new-rich said enviously to Floyd:

"I spend much more on my tailor than you do; you can afford to wear your old clothes."

Floyd smiled. He took in the young man—a fighting figure, physically strong, eager, on the alert, with gambler's eyes.

"You've never had to sweat blood for money."

The expression was coarse, but it threw a mental picture.

"No, I've never 'sweated blood' for a living."

"I didn't say a living, I said money. Any idiot can make a living. A man must have money and lots of it to be anybody; it's a hot game."

He wiped his forehead.

Floyd wondered if money could buy his armchair in the club-window. He was sure it couldn't, but he was a gentlemanly young fellow; he wouldn't hurt the man's feelings. Destiny had been more than kind to him. He wasn't grateful; he took life's favors as a matter of course. In fact, he never gave it any thought. When his father died, sorrow blunted the keen edge of existence; now after a year he was waking up. His heart's desire was Julie Gonzola. He had no fear; it was the eve of fulfillment.

Sitting there in the club-window, idly watching the traffic, he saw the Gonzola car. Julie was inside with Martin. They stopped at the entrance. Martin sprang out; Floyd waited for him with a pleasant touch of expectancy. Now there would be a long talk about Julie.

He came swinging in, his dark face quivering with excitement. Floyd didn't take Martin seriously; his unpleasant emotional nature gave his actions a touch of exaggeration, which repelled Floyd, with his calm, undisturbed nature.

"Well, why all this excitement? What's happened now?"

He spoke laughingly. Martin was always getting into some transient mix-up.

"I may as well tell you, you'll have to know it. I've asked Julie to marry me."

Floyd was on his feet, hurt, angry; Martin had listened hours to what he called "love ravings" about Julie, knowing he was waiting only for his year of mourning to expire. It was treachery. They faced each other—Martin had an air of triumph, but he turned away from Floyd's accusing eyes.

"I've given her twenty-four hours to prepare her mother."

"She'll not consent."

"Oh, won't she? I know the way to make her." Then he walked away.

9

Julie crouched in the corner of the car, her dark pupils contracting, dilating; she was going home to prepare her mother. The contempt in that letter she had written to Martin was awful, but she had promised and she braced herself for the fight. She was used to battles, bitter, uncompromising; used to the struggle of antagonistic spirits; but she had always been kept out of all that agony, pampered, spoilt, worshipped by her mother, indulged by her grandfather—and now she must fight them both, and she would. If they stood out against Martin, she would keep her word and go away with him; this was her determination. She stepped out of the car and found her mother waiting for her in the hall; she knew what was coming. Mrs. Gonzola led the way upstairs to her bedroom—watched Julie take off her hat and coat, and smooth down her hair.

"How long have you been meeting this man without my knowledge?"

"You mean Martin?"

"Yes."

"Since you forbade him the house."

"This is the first time in your life that you have openly disobeyed me. Why did you do it?"

"I love him, Mother, and he loves me, and I am going to marry him." She had rehearsed it in the car.

Mrs. Gonzola implored her not to marry that "ruffian" who had intrigued to get her affection. No man of honor would have acted like that. He was not the man for her—she was too young to realize it—she would hate him in the end. She begged, entreated her to wait a year. Julie burst into convulsed sobs.

"He won't wait, Mother—I've been through all that with him. Mother! Mother! Don't stop it, don't, I *must* marry him! I *must*!"

Mrs. Gonzola gave a terrible cry.

"What do you mean—tell me! Why must you marry him? Why?"

"Because! because!—he says he'll kill me if I don't."

Then Mrs. Gonzola warned her of the anger of Father Cabello, who would never marry her to an atheist, a heretic—warned her of her grandfather's curses (and the old Jew could curse); she heard him again, as he stood over her on the day of *her* marriage, pouring out his anger. His curses had come true in her wretched life, and this disobedient child—she was suffering as he had suffered that day—but now the old man was her only hope; Julie worshipped him. She threatened her with his anger, the wrath of the great Jewish God who does not forgive, who would bring down punishment upon her and her children's children.

The girl lay flat on the ground, quivering with horror, fear—then she became quite cold and stiff, and fell into a cataleptic trance, which lasted an hour. Mrs. Gonzola undressed her, put her into bed, and lay beside her, holding her close. The girl gradually grew warm, and smiled at her mother. The spasm of obstinacy over, she was again the submissive child. She would sacrifice herself and Martin, it was her duty; she became calm, almost cheerful, as was usual after those spells.

She wanted her mother to dress her as she did when she was a child. Mrs. Gonzola was happy; her life was bound up in this girl.

"You look so beautiful, Julie; go and show grandfather."

Mrs. Gonzola stood at the bottom of the stairs till Julie went in where Joseph Abravanel sat reading, unconscious of the tragedy which had been enacted below. He blessed her, called her a good child, the hope of his life. Then she and her mother dined in the big room with its dark Spanish tapestry and gold plate; it was a festive occasion. Mrs. Gonzola praised Floyd and his devotion to the memory of his father.

"You always liked him best as a child, didn't you, Julie?"

"No, Mother—I—I liked them *both*—" Then the fear came again of Martin!

"He will kill me, Mother. I'm afraid of him, afraid."

"Julie, I have no strength to fight for you. Marry Floyd; he is a simple honest boy. He has always loved you."

To her mother's great amazement Julie answered in slow deliberate tones—

"That will be the only way to save myself—but it must be at once. I mustn't have time to think about it—or I couldn't do it."

10

Floyd went home early that afternoon, stopping before the little gate. He had taken great pains with his garden. The lawn was velvety smooth; beds of flowers were banked up against the porch; geraniums bloomed in boxes at the windows. The polished brass knocker, the soft white curtain, gave the little house an atmosphere of purity, cleanliness. Passers stopped to admire it; they felt that "nice" people lived there.

Floyd shook off a sick feeling; anger nauseated him. The knocker gave out a musical call. The door was opened by a bright little Japanese boy—the old servants had gradually left during the lonely year of mourning. There was nothing changed in the house—the wood fire lit, the candles on the table set for two; he saw his father at the head of it. After dinner the boy brought his slippers and velvet house jacket. He stretched himself in a big chair and lit his pipe. He loved his pipe—that was the Knickerbocker strain in him; he smoked it with reverence as the old Dutchmen did—in the days when pipes were longer and tobacco better. He loved to sit before the wood fire, and listen to its hissing, crackling, singing; he thought of his mother's ancestors, those sturdy Pioneers in their cabins, piling on the logs, bolting their iron shutters against the howling wolves outside, who devoured the bodies and cracked the bones of men. The Puritans are gone, but the wolves are still with us; they eat the soul and sow wolf seed.

Then he thought how his father had planned his life for him, just as he had laid out his garden. It had not occurred to him that his son's life must be different from his own. His father's time was far away. Today things change with a flash—there is no more "slow development"—a fire!—a storm, lightning, ruins! He was a fool to be so sure of Julie; she had been very sympathetic in his year of mourning. He took it for love—Martin, that vulgarian, with his family history! He never had the slightest suspicion of what was going on between them. He'd been a blind fool.

He jumped to his feet; the clock struck ten. Twenty-four hours to prepare her mother. Why hadn't she said "No" at once and put an end to it? She couldn't want to marry him; it was unthinkable, but he never knew quite what she did think. When he said, "A penny for your thoughts," she grew very serious.

"My thoughts are only for myself."

He became impatient. Why make the thing so complicated? It was simple enough; they both wanted her and they'd have to fight for her as they did as boys. They never knew which of them she liked.

The telephone rang. He took up the receiver. It was Mrs. Gonzola's voice.

"Is it you, Floyd?"

"Yes."

"Could you come over for a few moments? It's late, but—"

"I'll come at once."

He stood before the mirror in the hall. It reflected a young man, clean-shaven, straight brows, eyes deep blue, almost black, the mouth set with suppressed pain; that was all the image gave out—nothing of the unsounded depths. The narcotic of ease and inherited aloofness had kept the lion of character sleeping.

Passing the Dillon house, Floyd noticed vaguely a sign "For Sale." Tom Dillon had inherited a large fortune which his father made in whiskey; he had boasted he would drink up the well-stocked cellar before he got rid of the house. It was illuminated tonight; he heard music and loud laughter; Tom was on the job.

In the parlor of the Gonzola mansion the butler pressed a button which lit up the unaccountable glass prisms of the electrified fixture; it was a familiar room. As a boy, its grandeur had awed him; when he grew older, he thought it old-fashioned, but he didn't want to see it changed. He knew little of the other part of the house, excepting the dining-room which was in old leather, heavy, dark. He had always spoken with superiority of the "charming Spanish atmosphere" of the room. Tonight it struck him differently. "What an ignorant fool he was." A man who mentally kicks himself for being all kinds of a fool is often awakening to wisdom.

The floor was parquet, smooth and polished. There were Oriental rugs and deep armchairs, upholstered in Turkish, and a broad divan with wonderful silk rugs thrown over it. Fur animals lay about with enormous heads and glassy eyes. The window hangings were of costly lace. He had often looked at that bronze figure in a corner; tonight it spoke to him. It was the Moses of Michael Angelo—a noble head with a rippling, flowing beard. The walls were covered with family portraits in gilt frames, turning old gold with age. He had said with authority "they are Van Dykes." Now he noticed signed names unknown to him, probably young foreign artists. He stood before a portrait of Pedro Gonzola, Julie's grandfather, painted in Amsterdam, after a ball costume. A very handsome young cavalier in black velvet with white lace falling over his long, tapering fingers—he thought of Martin's coarse hands; no, the room was not Spanish.

Mrs. Gonzola came in; she, too, took on a new significance; a woman of fifty, small, sinuous, with pale eyelids, forehead, lips; the process of Time had almost washed out the human face which had been, even at its best, but a soft water-color.

Tonight Floyd seemed to see within that white Image. Past struggles, like smothered flames, flashed up again momentarily. Her English was perfect—so academic it sounded foreign; born in New York, taught by professors, she spoke like one. She had tried to bring Julie up that way, but changed conditions were too strong for her.

"Floyd, I am in a terrible dilemma. Martin has asked Julie to marry him."

"Yes, I know."

She tried to draw away her hands, but Floyd held them fast.

"Your decision means everything to me." Floyd put his arm around her; he had known her all his life. She clung to him; there were tears in her voice, but her eyes were dry.

"Julie told you of our ancestry?"

"Yes."

"Does it make any difference?"

"Why should it?"

An evasive answer. Why didn't he make it simple, and say "No"?

"Some people are prejudiced, but you have no family ties, and are not religious. I don't want Julie to marry Martin, he's vulgar; they are peasants, common cattle drivers; his grandfather was a waiter—I can't think of it, it's too horrible!"

Floyd tried to be fair.

"But if Julie likes him better—"

"She does not; I'm sure of it. She is very impressionable. Martin has a kind of brute force; you know him. He'll talk her into it. It will be a terrible misfortune for her; it will ruin her life! I must make it impossible; I must!"

Floyd was speechless with excitement. She had her arms around him, clinging to him.

"Julie is a strange girl, at the mercy of inherited instincts—she will be safe with you."

Why did she say that? What was wrong with Julie? Floyd began to take Julie's part against her mother.

"Mrs. Gonzola, be calm, I beg of you. You know I have wanted Julie all my life; you know I want her now. If she loves Martin better, what—what—can I do?"

"No, no, she will tell you herself," Mrs. Gonzola glided out of the room. Floyd wiped his forehead. What did it all mean? Why was she so afraid of Martin? What was he doing there, anyhow? Martin had been open with him, now *he* was conspiring with her mother. No, he would do nothing underhand. He would give Martin a chance to get his answer as agreed. Julie must be free to choose.

She stood in the doorway. He wanted to tell her what was in his mind, but she didn't give him time. She came straight to him, put her arms around his neck; her soft body intoxicated him. His heart's desire realized—Julie his wife; he couldn't let her go, he kissed her again and again. She laughed and said in her soft, sensuous voice:

"Oh, oh, don't eat me."

"It's forever, Julie, forever?"

He stammered out the words. He was terribly excited, poor lad. She grew very serious.

"Yes—it is forever." Then she cried and he tried to comfort her.

"I've had a great deal of excitement today. Go now."

She let him kiss her again. He went unsteadily like a soberly inclined man who had rushed violently into an orgy of liquor. It was dawn when he slipped quietly out of his house and dropped a letter to Martin into the post-box, he had written everything, just how it happened.

The only thing that clouds my indescribable happiness is the thought that you may resent my not giving you your chance, but it was out of my hands. When Mrs. Gonzola called me tonight, I had no idea of what was awaiting me. My happiness came to me. I cannot let it go.

He expected no answer to his letter. It came by return mail:

There is nothing to be angry about; I would have done the same in your place. I would take her away from you now, if it were possible, but—don't be uneasy, she doesn't care enough for me. I don't think she's insane about you, but you are the safer proposition. You won't see me for some time.

Martin had a way of disappearing when things went against him. Floyd read the letter once more. "The safer proposition." Of course, she would be safe with him; he was too happy to let the significance of a word worry him. He slowly tore the letter in little pieces, and said nothing to Julie about it.

The next evening, he went over to dine with the Gonzolas. Mrs. Gonzola had asked him quietly not to come during the day.

"Julie needs time to calm down."

"Calm down?" laughed Floyd. "It's too early for that."

"She is quite exhausted. She must get used to the idea."

It was not exhausting to him to get used to happiness. It came natural to think of Julie as "my dear wife." He saw many, many years ahead. As they grew old they would get fonder of each other, like his mother and father. A pang shot through him; if they were alive now! He had not "lived" like other men; he had waited for the one woman. The close contact was intoxicating, leaving him incapable of logical reasoning. He waited impatiently for the evening.

Julie stood under the big chandelier; her soft white gown with a touch of red velvet seemed a part of her flexible body; a filet of it was drawn over her forehead. Her full red lips were a splash of color in her pale face. She came quite naturally to him; Floyd's heart beat furiously. Mrs. Gonzola looked regal in black lace, relieved by a huge diamond brooch set in old silver. She approved of Floyd; he was a gentleman.

"My father lives with us. Julie has probably told you; I want her to take you up to see him. Don't speak of your engagement yet. Julie will break it to him gradually, but I want him to know you, and I am sure he will love you as we do."

How gracious she was; it was like the condescension of a Queen.

"Break it to him," as if it were bad news. Floyd felt uncomfortable.

Julie led the way up to the fourth floor. They entered a very large room with mullion windows; one, at the extreme end, of yellow glass. He was conscious of warmth, a glory of golden sunlight, the odor of a hothouse, many palms. Under a tropical tree with enormous leaves spread out like an umbrella sat a man with a black silk skull cap on his head. He was absorbed in his book. He did not raise his eyes. Floyd at a first glance caught the impression of age, because of a long thick white beard, falling in waves, turning up at the edges in curls, which reminded him of Michael Angelo's Moses, but *this* statue lived. Julie spoke very respectfully. She seemed in awe of him.

"Grandfather, I've brought Floyd Garrison to see you."

He arose and came toward Floyd. He wore a long black silk coat reaching to his ankles, with velvet collar, cuffs, and slippers. His feet were very small, his hands like a woman's; the voice which came from that frail body was clear, penetrating.

"My name is Joseph Abravanel."

His eyes were young. Floyd felt himself being measured and weighed, but that didn't disturb him; he had no secrets.

"I know all about you, Floyd. I've watched you grow up. That little snowball fight with Martin twelve years ago this winter was fine. You were small; but you buried him." He laughed like a boy. Floyd sat down beside him, listening intensely; he didn't want to lose a word. Julie flittered about the room, watching them.

"I like you, Floyd; you're a good fighter."

"Oh, no," laughed Floyd, "I'm a pacifist."

The old man shook his head.

"Wait, you haven't found yourself yet. We Jews are fighters, although the world says we are not. We've been fighting for thousands of years."

Then he spoke of the possibilities of America joining the War.

"It will come; we will be forced into it. We Jews will get the worst of it as usual, but that's good for us; the will to live becomes stronger."

He continually repeated "we Jews" as if to impress the fact of his race upon Floyd.

"The American aliens will find relatives in every European field of battle; it will be terrible, like the Civil War, brother against brother."

Floyd had never thought of it that way.

"The Jews are like an old tree—its branches spread all over the world; it roots are in the Bible. The Arian education is Greek, opposite to that of the Hebrew. The Greeks worshipped form, beauty; its idols were in stone. The Hebrews rejected that; they based their religion on the 'Word.' You see? the body, the Soul; the Image Greek, the Soul Hebrew."

After that, Floyd found his way often to the fourth floor. He heard many things foreign to his way of thinking, but of deep interest to him.

"Now," said Floyd laughingly one evening, "I've made myself popular with all the family."

"No," answered Julie, "there is one more, Father Cabello."

11

Father Cabello was an indispensable part of the Gonzola family, from the Celtic help in the kitchen, to the aristocratic old man on the top floor, whose guest he was on Friday evenings, when he shared a simple meal of vegetables and fruit, washed down with a glass of delicious Palestinian wine; after that, a game of chess, and a long theological discussion which lasted many a time until the small hours. The two men, of the same origin but of different creeds, understood each other perfectly. When it came to a burning question, such as the sincerity of Paul—whether his hatred of the High Priests of Judea had not instigated him to dethrone them, by putting another in their place, one he had never seen, or whether it was an inspiration, "a voice out of the wilderness"—then Joseph Abravanel's eyes took on a fiery gleam. Father

Cabello, seeing the danger signal, would evade the question by a witty remark, ending with a laugh. Julie gave Floyd a hint. He invited the good Father to lunch with him at the club.

He sat in the window watching the priest shaking hands with one and the other—a man of Church and World, known to rich and poor, and generally beloved. Floyd had a feeling of embarrassment, but Father Cabello put him at once in smooth waters by a remark about the "exclusive policy" of the club.

"Yes," answered Floyd. "This distinction against aliens is very reactionary." He forgot he was on the membership committee before he was engaged; then he ventured to say:

"I—I am very glad you do not oppose my marriage with Julie."

"Why should I?"

He knew Floyd was not a Catholic; why did he make him emphasize that?

"I was prepared for your opposition on account of my religion."

The priest smiled.

"The man who fights the inevitable destroys no one but himself. I have had one great battle in that family; I don't want a second—if—it can be avoided. When Julie was born, her mother and I together fought and conquered Joseph Abravanel; a fine fellow, deeply learned. In the great days of the Church in Spain, he would have been a distinguished Cardinal." The priest puffed regretfully at his cigar. "His ancestors were foolishly fanatic; they chose the evil of emigration to the glory of power and the Pope."

Floyd answered eagerly.

It was a question of principle; they should be admired, respected, for such noble self-sacrifice.

The priest liked the boy; there was no complication to fight in him.

"This marriage was a question of you and one other. I chose you."

Floyd's face grew hot. It had all been arranged between the mother and the priest.

"Then you considered me the lesser of two evils?"

The priest smiled again.

"You are not an evil, you are a concession; we make them, if they do not bring us future harm; the children will be ours, but don't let it worry you now."

- 26 -

"Pedro Gonzola's marriage with a Jewess was also a concession. Why did you allow *that?*"

"This boy is no fool," thought the priest; he took pains to answer the question.

"We were mistaken in our calculations, we *are* sometimes; we remained passive because we were sure Joseph Abravanel would fight it with all his might; and he did. But another power mightier than he and the Church together won out; the strongest combination in the world—youth and love. Ruth was his only child, she threatened to leave him, he worshipped her, he had to give in, but he went to live with the young couple, with a firm resolve to counteract our influence. The inevitable happened; she came to us for consolation. Julie was born in the church."

They were silent. The priest lived again that interesting conflict. The old man had fought well, he was wonderful with his unanswerable arguments, but reason went down under the great emotional rising of the soul—the need of forgiveness.

Floyd's voice brought him back.

"Why did he remain in his daughter's house?"

"Because with the obstinate patience of his race, he had hopes of Julie's children." Then he bent nearer, lowering his voice. "There is something else you should know. From the day Julie was baptized, Joseph Abravanel has never seen or spoken to his daughter."

The atmosphere of tragedy folded itself about Floyd; he felt the clashing of spiritual powers, within the walls of that outwardly peaceful home, now creeping like slow fire into his life.

12

Near Floyd's house, there was a small stone chapel ornamented with dark wooden beams; it had been built by Mr. Garrison and Mr. Steele. They brought over their pastor from Scotland, a rugged, sincere man.

Floyd still grew chilly, when he thought of the bare whitewashed walls, the stone floor, the hard wooden benches. No choir, no organ, no stained glass windows. The pastor generally took his text from one of those Hebrew "calamity howlers," and hurled curses at the heads of his unfortunate parishioners. He was a man of mild disposition, but he thought it was his duty to snatch them from the worship of Mammon. The "Idolaters" would listen meekly, rise, sing a hymn, and file out penitently, to pursue on week days, their ungodly practices.

In course of time the pastor went to heaven, his congregation the other way; Martin said it might be the reverse. Other pastors modified their curses or ceased to hurl them; the times demanded blessings, and paid for them. The congregation grew rich and moved uptown. Floyd kept his pew out of respect for his parents.

He told the pastor, a sensible man from the West with a large growing family, of his coming marriage.

"We are not losing you; we lost you when your father died. Of course, you must consider the bride's family; the women generally arrange those matters, but I would like to come and see you sometimes. Your children may in course of time think differently."

He, also, had hopes of the next generation.

Now Floyd pushed away all unpleasant thoughts; his youth demanded happiness. He went up the steps of the Gonzola mansion with a light heart, humming to himself. The butler ushered him into the dimly lighted parlor. He waited, but Julie did not come. He heard voices above. He was one of the family now by right of knowing all its secrets. He found Julie crouched at the bottom of the upper stairs; at the door of the old man's room was Mrs. Gonzola on her knees. Floyd tried to question Julie, but she silenced him with an imperative gesture.

The voices of Father Cabello and Joseph Abravanel, penetrating the closed door, rang throughout the house. Floyd heard his name; it was a question of his marriage with Julie, of the ceremony, and again, those future generations. He heard the deep tones of the priest—threatening, persuasive; the other voice trembling, feeble, rising in a despairing shriek, dying away in sobs. It was terrible; every word seemed to strike that prostrate figure at the door like a whip. Floyd thought of the rack. The priest came out wiping his forehead, he lifted the stricken woman; the Church had won again.

They were married quietly at home, the bride in old lace and priceless family jewels, a vision of Oriental beauty. Martin's words came back to Floyd. "To me she is not a modern girl, she is the Shulamite maiden who rises from her couch at night and goes out to seek her lover."

Floyd wanted to bring his wife to the house where he was born; Julie gladly consented. He had been so dear, giving in to everybody, for the sake of peace. At the door of his home, Floyd took Julie up in his arms and carried her over the threshold as his fathers had done before him.

13

The young couple were called home from a brief trip, by the sudden death of Joseph Abravanel.

Julie's grief was terrible. She stood by the plain deal coffin where he lay in his shroud, looking long at the marble face. Floyd felt her suffering, but he was powerless to console her. He wondered why Mrs. Gonzola kept her room; she surely would want to say good-bye to her father. He turned; she was there; she entered slowly, as if in fear. Julie made a quick step forward.

The voice that came from Mrs. Gonzola's white lips was red with the blood of her race.

"I must see him."

"You dare not."

"Have pity on me."

"I promised him to keep you away."

"He will not know."

"He will know, he must rest in peace."

They were not mother and daughter; they were enemies.

Mrs. Gonzola turned and went downstairs in silence. She died a few days later without breaking that silence.

Joseph Abravanel had given away what little he possessed during his lifetime; to Julie he left a small Hebrew prayer book, worn with age. Mrs. Gonzola's will was complicated. She had given generously to the Church for years. Julie was to have the house and contents and the income of what was left, the capital going to the grandchildren on condition of their fidelity to the Church; otherwise it went to support a theological seminary in Rome.

They were standing together in the parlor. The room was icy; her face, pinched, worn.

"I am going to sell the house and everything in it."

"What! Sell your family portraits?"

"I've had enough of them, persecuting me with their angry faces. They despise me; I feel it. I have felt it all my life; as a child I saw them in my dreams coming out of their frames threatening me! I am done with them, done with them!" She broke into convulsive sobs. She took him by the hand, and led him around the room, stopping before each one of her childhood's inquisitors.

"Do you want to live with them all your life?"

"No, I certainly do not—but—"

"I'll have them packed up and sent back to the family in Europe who will hang them in their picture galleries. We have none...."

The sight of Julie in lustreless black and a long crêpe veil made Floyd shudder; it was awful. Black obscured her beauty, she spoke in low tones, went around on tip-toe. There was the silence of death in his house.

"I can't stand this, Julie. We're living as in a cemetery; it's getting on my nerves. How long is it going to last?"

"One year."

Floyd didn't like to appear heartless, but he had already learnt to use a little diplomacy with his wife.

"Do you realize how unbecoming black is to you?"

She looked at him, startled.

"It is my duty to wear it."

"It's gone out of fashion. Only old people wear crêpe nowadays; a black band is quite sufficient. Why should you parade your grief?"

She didn't answer, but the next morning she came to breakfast in a "royal" purple tea gown.

Floyd kissed her eyes, lips, hands; he had his sweetheart again.

Julie smiled at him. She liked to be worshipped.

"Come, come! I'm hungry. Don't you want any breakfast?"

"I want nothing but you."

The Japanese laid the morning paper on the table and discreetly withdrew. Floyd looking over the headings, sprang to his feet.

"War?"

Julie gave a startled cry.

"You won't go, you won't leave me alone."

"I must do my duty."

He went down to see Colonel Garland. The office was in a whirl of excitement. The Colonel was prancing like an old war horse. Everybody was talking at once. It had to come; the President had put it off too long; some were for, some against it, but the fact was there—the United States had thrown her hat into the ring. Floyd's face was flushed, his eyes shining.

"I'm going to volunteer."

The Colonel looked grave.

"Wait, let the single men go first."

Floyd couldn't be held back; every man he knew had volunteered. He met Tom Dillon with a little flag stuck in his buttonhole, his hat set jauntily on the side of his head.

"I'm going into camp tomorrow."

That night there was a scene with Julie; she begged, cried, fainted. Dr. McClaren was sent for, the diagnosis was—Motherhood. Floyd did not volunteer.

All New York crowded the streets to bid Godspeed to the first regiment sailing for France. "Our Boys" with flowers in their caps, flowers stuck in their guns marched proudly. The people went mad.

Floyd, holding Julie tightly, stood on the corner of Fifth Avenue. He had a feeling of depression; for the first time in his life a wish had been thwarted. He looked down at the curly head with its sport-hat pressed close to his arm, noticed the glances of admiration. She was worth the sacrifice. Suddenly with a well-directed aim, she flung a rose at a passing soldier. He caught it, pressed it to his lips with a long glance backward.

"That was Martin," said Julie.

They walked home in silence. Julie had a headache from the noise and excitement and went to bed early.

Floyd sat up; he tried to think of Julie and the future. He couldn't; the cheers were still in his ears, the tramping of feet, the clashing of cymbals. He sat there, out of it. Love was cruel....

The boy was christened by Father Cabello, his last service to the Gonzola family. He had been called to Rome, where honors awaited him, for his services to the Church in America.

"What name are you going to give him?" asked the Father.

Julie, lying in her white bed, answered:

"His name will be Joseph Abravanel Gonzola Garrison."

Floyd thought it too high-sounding for modern times—an American citizen couldn't carry it, but Julie had her way.

After Father Cabello's departure, she went seldom to the Cathedral and gradually ceased altogether.

"I've lived all my life under the tyranny of two religions. My boy must be free of that; when he is old enough he will choose for himself." But she still read her grandfather's little Hebrew book at night when she couldn't sleep, or when she awoke terrified from the reality of her dreams. She never spoke of it to Floyd, and he didn't like to intrude.

BOOK II

"The Present—gray tones of actuality—A moving picture.

Crowds struggling—Shattered Ideals—Truth in danger."

BOOK II

1

MARTIN STEELE came back to America after two years' absence. He was known over there as the "Yankee Devil." Danger seemed to attract him; he rushed through a rain of bullets and planted the flag in the face of the enemy. He was happy; the straining of nerve and sinew helped to quiet an inward restlessness. On landing he found a telegram from his mother; she wanted him to go up and see "The Museum" before coming to Boston. He tore up the telegram with an ugly scowl.

The corner of Broadway and Forty-second Street—gigantic waves of humanity passing, moving up, down, across—screeching automobiles emitting pestilential odors—rapidly changing electric signs—the only stagnation was in the air—it weighed on his chest, halted his breath. He stood with his hands deep in his pockets. There was something psychic going on within him; the boys who came home brought with them a strange consciousness: they had seen miracles.

He felt the leaden mentality oozing out from the crowd, became keenly conscious of the mixture of races; those tense, strained faces, looking straight ahead; the past forgotten; the future—who cares? "We build for today; the next man will build for his day." "The Present" in electric letters of colored flames. "How am I to borrow or steal for—women—for wine. Prohibition?—ha! ha!—who takes that seriously; who takes anything seriously?"

Martin elbowed himself through the crowd; a soldier in khaki, people looked after him; a fine strong fellow from the prairies, seeing the sight of the Great White Way.

He mopped his forehead, saying to himself, "Where shall I go?"

He stood before the house where he was born, read the black and gold sign on the door.

"The Winthrop Museum. Tuesday, Thursday, Saturday (admission free); other days fifty cents." It was Friday.

The sleepy official handed him a card. Martin threw down his fifty cents and entered. There were a few stragglers strolling from case to case, mostly strangers. A large omnibus, "Seeing New York," waited outside; the man on the box blew the horn.

"This is the house of the celebrated Winthrop family whose ancestors came over in the *Mayflower*. The owners have generously donated their historical relics to the city; ten minutes allowed for inspection."

He looked at the old furniture, falling to pieces from want of repair; some were really family relics, but the parading of them—"who cares for other people's old sticks"? The caretaker was putting on his hat to go when Martin spoke to him.

"I'm Mr. Steele. I'm going to close up this dugout." He put ten dollars in the man's hand. With one strong wrench he tore down the sign, locked the door, and put the key in his pocket.

He stopped before the Garrison home; it was lit up inside. He opened the gate, shut it with a sharp click, and went up toward Fifth Avenue. The row of small brick houses were in a sorry plight. On Maud Ailsworth's window there was a sign, "Table Board"; on the Gonzola mansion, "For Sale." "The mother and grandfather dead, Julie married." Then he bought the biggest basket of red roses he could find, and followed on the heels of the messenger.

Floyd was in the nursery, revelling in the beauty of mother and child—a wonderful Murillo picture. Julie laughed at his caressing epithets, "Two angels to take care of"—etc., etc., and all the rest a man like Floyd would naturally say to the young mother of his child. She went to dinner leaning on his arm. Julie was one of the rare women who become beautiful with motherhood; from the first moment of its consciousness, she was a changed being. The grief and horror of her double misfortune vanished; her eyes became larger, more brilliant. The dead white of her skin changed into a soft pink; the rippling hair shone, getting more and more rebellious, escaping in soft curls about her face.

She gave a cry of pleasure at the roses on the table.

"Oh! how gorgeous! Floyd, you mustn't spoil me like this."

"I didn't send them."

"You didn't?"

"No, my word of honor."

"Then who? I can't think of anyone, unless—"

"Who?"

She fastened a rose in her dress, forgetting to answer.

The table was faultlessly set with fine damask. The heavy cut glass sparkled in the candle light. A pine wood fire threw a soft glimmer over the room; there was no other light. Floyd felt a sense of æsthetic satisfaction. He hated the big flats of the West Side with their electric illumination; he was glad he didn't have to live in them. The bell rang.

"Who can that be at this hour?"

"You needn't announce me, I'll go right in."

"Martin!"

Julie was on her feet looking for a way of escape. Floyd put her back in her seat.

"Stay where you are."

Floyd's hand went out to meet Martin's; he'd come back from the front, and they had known each other all their lives.

"I landed today. I feel like a stranger in a foreign land. Will you let me have a bite with you?"

He hadn't changed; heavily tanned; a little more muscular; a little louder. He grasped Julie's hand, and held it fast. There was a slight heaving under the red rose; her cheeks had lost their color. He absorbed everything with those eyes of his. She felt the loose gown hanging from her shoulders, and drew it around her full bosom. He turned to Floyd, with a laughing question in his eyes. Floyd laughed back; he couldn't help feeling a sense of triumph.

Martin was very entertaining, told amusing stories in French; there was something pathetic in his efforts to please. Julie took a childish delight in his medals. Floyd's face clouded over; Martin took them from her hand.

"They mean nothing to me."

"You should be proud of them," insisted Julie. "They are a reward for bravery. You were brave. We read about you."

"I wouldn't give the others the satisfaction of thinking me a coward."

"But you were afraid at first; it's only natural."

He turned and looked straight at her.

"No. What is there in life for me? It takes more courage to go on living."

There was a long pause; Julie arose, said "good night." Floyd went with her to the stairs, kissed her; Martin's eyes followed them. Then Floyd threw himself into the big chair by the fire, forgetting everything but the dear woman, the dear child.

Martin sat puffing at his pipe; it was foul. Julie couldn't bear a pipe. Floyd had given up his then he shut the door carefully, lit his pipe laughingly, saying something about a bad example. He was eager for more stories of war, carnage, murder.

"A wonderful experience. I envy you."

"Why didn't you go?"

"I couldn't leave Julie in her condition."

There was a silence; then Martin spoke in a hard voice which conveyed repression.

"Your experience has been more wonderful than mine."

He threw down his pipe, pacing the room, muttering broken sentences; there was a strange glitter in his eyes. He cursed everything, everybody.

"Patriotism, bah! We punched holes in that lie, sitting in our dugout waiting for the death call. Love of the soil; bah! I was born next door; another year you also will be driven out. Our children won't even know the spot where their parents lived; what does it matter, anyhow? The farmer, bah! He values the soil as he does his cow, for what he can get out of it; it isn't *his* land. He came over, bought it, because he couldn't steal it, mortgaged it, misused it. The boys won't go back to the farm. They want money, they'll get it the next few years. The rest of the world will starve—America will wallow in the filthy stuff—not you, nor I—we're pikers, that's what we are; our fathers thought they left us rich; I could plunge in, reconstruct, sell out, gamble with my money, and make a fortune. What then?" He stood glaring at Floyd, a desperate, hopeless creature, Martin's ravings always depressed him; Julie's voice broke the oppressive silence.

"Floyd, bring Martin up to see the baby."

He stood in the doorway like a bashful boy, Floyd put the child in his arms; he looked down at the little dark head against his arm, bent and kissed it, giving Julie a look of lightning rapidity. It scorched her.

Martin became a frequent visitor at the Garrisons', running in often at inopportune moments.

Julie was sitting over the fire in the dining-room, the child asleep in a little pink-lined basket beside her. She leaned back; there was a feeling of lassitude, weariness; she had every reason to be happy; no woman could ask more; but why that longing to get away from her child, her husband, from herself? Why did she feel the walls of her life? She knew there was something wrong with her; she felt too intensely. Martin! Why had he come back? She was happy with Floyd; he was good, gentle; kind, so different; but Martin! Martin!

She heard his voice outside, she must get upstairs; she went swiftly to the door—too late—he was in the room taking her in with those terrible eyes.

"Why did you break in like this? It's very inconsiderate. I am not fit to see strangers."

"Strangers, Julie!"

She raised her arms above her head, twisting the thick ropes of falling hair, trying to fasten them. Her shawl fell away, disclosing the corsetless form, the open neck.

Waves of passion rushed through him.

"Don't go! Give me one moment more, just one!" He caught at her shawl. A terrible shame burnt her. She staggered out, slamming the door after her. Martin pressed the shawl, warm from her body, to his face; the hot tears rolled down.

He didn't come again for some time. One day Floyd met him at the club.

"Why don't we see you at the house? We miss you."

Martin's eyes had a look of abstraction.

"Your home is like a nest just now. There is room in it only for two—and the little bird." It was a beautiful thought; but that humor never lasted long with him. He said abruptly:

"I've sold my house. They are going to build a skyscraper. It will take away your light."

Floyd's face darkened.

"That won't drive us out."

"Why stay there? You can get a big profit."

"I was born there; I want to die there."

Martin laughed mockingly.

"A man who dies in the house where he was born should be ticketed and put into a museum."

2

The wreckers were at work tearing down the Steele house. Floyd, passing, found Martin in overalls, his hair, face, eyelashes, white with plaster dust, his tongue swinging with the hammer.

"You obstinate devil, I'll show you who is the master."

The wall was well built, too well; in the old days they built for the future. He gave it a blow, another, another; it didn't yield. He worked himself into a purple rage. Blow after blow fell upon the unhappy partition; it trembled, the others jumped away; it fell. Martin stood triumphantly among the ruins.

Floyd's eyes grew moist. Was there no feeling in the man? Did he realize he had made himself homeless? Now he must join the rich tramps, the poor tramps, that army of wanderers living here awhile, there awhile, places to sleep and eat; luxurious, tawdry, squalid imitations, according to their money value. New York was becoming a homeless city.

He related the incident to Julie.

"Martin looks seedy, he neglects his appearance, he's a forsaken wretch."

Julie had a sudden inspiration.

"I'm going to get him married."

Floyd laughed.

"It takes two for that."

Julie stood before her mirror; a pleasing picture flashed back. A smooth young face—not a trace of the physical agony she had been through, of the mental agony; her life was running now along smooth, conventional lines—a beautiful woman, bending forward, studying her expression. Is there a telltale line? No; the mask fits to the life.

"May I come in?"

It was Maud Ailsworth invited to dinner to meet Martin. Julie was going to see what she could do. Maud's mother had been dead four years; she had known her only as an invalid propped up by pillows, with an ice bag on her head. Maud left school early to take the housekeeping, which was a sorry job, in her hands. Mrs. Ailsworth's philosophy of living was that good things were cheapest in the end. The modest capital left by her husband melted, they sold the house, and lived on the money. When Mrs. Ailsworth died, Maud had five thousand dollars. She took a room on the top floor rear of a fashionable hotel, and spent her time looking for a husband. She wanted a nice man, she would wait another year; and then—there was always Tom Dillon. She didn't have to act with him. He knew she was a beggar, she knew he was a rotter;

but she wouldn't do it until her last penny was gone. She still had hopes of someone better. She was pretty, quick with an answer, and much liked by men, but—they didn't marry her.

"Why?"

She asked herself that question many a night, after a party, where the men went the limit. There *she* stopped; the other girls jumped the boundaries. She wondered if that was why she was single at twenty-five. Well, she couldn't; it wasn't her virtue, it was her misfortune.

She noticed at a first glance how much prettier Julie had become, but she didn't compliment her. It wasn't her way.

"You have had a hard time, haven't you?"

"Yes, but it's worth all I suffered."

Maud's nostrils expanded, taking in the subtle essence of violet powder.

"Oh! I *smell* the baby."

She flew to the crib and took the child in her arms.

"You handle it like a grandmother!" cried Julie. "Why don't you get married?"

Maud laughed mirthlessly.

"Why? Because the only man I really want won't ask me; it's your fault, Julie—one wasn't enough for you."

"How can you say that?"

"What are you going to do with the other?" insisted Maud.

Julie answered with a touch of seriousness.

"I am going to get him for you, if I can. Do you like him?"

Maud spoke slowly, weighing her words.

"Liking is too neutral for Martin Steele; it is either love or hate; I think I hate him." She gave a quick glance into the mirror as they went down to dinner.

The men were waiting in the parlor. Martin was ill at ease; he felt like a waiter in evening dress. Floyd wore it differently; he melted into it. Maud as the guest of honor was charming. All laughed heartily at her frank admissions, and keen enjoyment of the fruits so long forbidden.

"We've got a free hand. Politically, economically; the right to work—"

"You can have it," interrupted Martin. "I'll give you my share."

"But we want more—Moral Equality."

"Isn't that a step backward?" said Floyd. "Until now, women were supposed to be morally superior to men."

"Why should they be? Equal rights is all we want. We are no longer going to be 'cast out' for acting naturally."

Martin took up the gauntlet.

"You mean you want to have children without being married?"

Maud's eyes shot defiance.

"Yes, that's what I mean."

"Haven't you taken that privilege?"

"I? Not yet, but I don't know what I may do."

It was getting too personal, Julie arose from the table. Floyd lingered with Martin.

"She doesn't mean a word of all that. She's a fine woman; she'll make a good wife and mother."

Martin blew rings of smoke into the air.

"I'm quite sure she will, but I'm not interested."

Maud was curled up in an armchair by the fire, one leg under her, the other hanging down; she was smoking a cigarette in a gold-mounted amber holder.

Julie put her arm in Floyd's.

"Let's go and say good night to baby."

Martin smiled at her transparent subterfuge. He looked down at Maud; a well-shaped head, correct features, eyes curious; the black stuff she used gave them the requisite look of the demi-mondaine. The glass beads around her neck were cheap; what there was of the gown was evidently designed and put together by herself. Her thin silk stockings were going in the seams; he was sure there were holes in the feet. He'd like to dress her well. Yes, she was a nice girl; he could easily be single with her for six months—but marriage?

Julie's laugh rang out upstairs. Maud was conscious of being checked up.

"Well, what's the verdict?"

"Will you let me say what I think?"

"Yes, if you let me do the same."

"You will say more than you believe, I less."

There was something fascinating in the fellow's insolence.

"Legs, neck, shoulders, bust, perfect; the symmetry of thighs and limbs—classic; but you leave me cold."

"Why?" She bent over with a touch of eagerness.

"Because there is nothing of mystery about you."

"Ha, ha; why should a woman be a mystery?"

Then came a flash which revealed depths unsounded.

"Because all holy things are mysterious; when a woman ceases to be holy to man, she kills love in him."

Maud wouldn't argue on those lines.

"Other men don't think so."

"They do. Have you ever been inside the Museum of Art in Central Park?"

"Oh, yes, I've been to the receptions."

"Will you come with me to see the pictures and statues?"

"I'll go anywhere with you."

He sat on the arm of her chair.

"You will find in some of the mutilated Grecian goddesses the same length of limbs and lines of body; but they are modestly undraped—"

"Stop. I don't like that expression; I believe in leaving something to the imagination."

"A man's imagination in that respect is a vile thing."

"I never thought of it that way."

"Think of it that way, will you?"

"Yes."

It slipped out; she was sorry at once, but she didn't recall it.

"When I look at the girl of today, I feel that I am passing with the rest of the crowd before those wonderful marble statues, which belong to everyone, to *no one.*"

She was on her feet now blazing at him.

"How dare you demand purity in us? Set the example; we'll follow suit. We give what we receive; no more, no less."

She made a rush for the door. He caught her two arms.

"You women! You women! You prate equality; you'd hate like the devil to have it. You know you've got the best of us." Martin's voice rang out; it was always too loud when he was excited. "The woman of today is gambling with every chance against her; if she wins, she loses; she'll get everything she wants, even sexual equality; and when she has it, she'll lose the glory of Life for the human race. Look at me. I'm the average man, no better, no worse; and the most miserable, lonely wretch that ever walked in a city overcrowded with beautiful women. I would marry any one of them—high, low, rich, poor, if she would give me the love I'm craving for. Tell me the truth now: can you love anybody but yourself?"

She tried to extricate herself from his iron grasp, his accusing eyes.

"Don't, don't! You hurt me."

He released her with a bitter laugh.

When Julie came in, Maud was hysterical. Martin must have been saying something awful.

The Japanese announced:

"Miss Ailsworth's car."

"Oh! Have you a car?" exclaimed Julie.

"It belongs to Tom Dillon; he wants me to keep his chauffeur busy." She was herself again, saucy, reckless, unthinking.

Martin bent over her, speaking in low tones.

"I'll go home with you; we'll make up on the way."

She knew what he meant—she'd show him—he couldn't love *her* for the moment.

"I don't want you; a man's escort is not a guarantee of safety."

She kissed Julie and swept out, followed by Floyd. He stood at the door of the car; there was something wrong with Maud. He thought he saw tears in her eyes. He jumped into the car and went home with her. Julie was at the window as they drove off.

"Oh! Floyd's gone with her. He's so old-fashioned; he hates to see women roaming about alone at night; he won't be long."

She pulled down the blinds, put out the lights, leaving only the candles and the glow of the fire.

Martin stood watching her. She began to feel uncomfortable. Why didn't he say something? She was afraid of his silence.

"Maud's a nice girl, and very popular. I wonder why she doesn't marry."

He answered roughly.

"I'm not going to marry her; drop that idea, will you."

He came close to her, leaning against the side-board.

"You're disappointed?"

"I? Oh, no."

"Confess." He put his hand under her chin, and forced her to look at him. "You want to get rid of me?"

"Yes. I do."

"Why? Tell me!"

In the half light, her face was like ivory. Her eyes shone back into his. He started, and put his hand on her shoulder; what was it he saw there? She came closer to him, closer; he dared not move. She kissed him again, again, murmuring soft love words. Then he broke out, held her as if he would never let her go, calling her his beautiful Queen, his Oriental Pearl, his Song of Songs. She clung to him, her body responding to his; how long?—a moment, which goes back centuries, a century which is only a moment. He felt her tears on his face, as she caressed and kissed him; every drop of blood in him answered.

"I wanted you always. You know it—you know it. I thought the longing would wear away with time; my mother said it would. I believed her; but she lied to me, lied! It was always there, getting more and more unbearable."

Martin closed her lips with a long kiss. This wonderful tempting, seductive creature; he would never let her go.

"I wanted you to marry Maud to save myself. When I saw you with her tonight, the pain was unbearable. I couldn't go on—I couldn't." Then she drew away from him, and went over to the fire, her hands clasped together, her face convulsed; the red light enveloped her.

He came to her. She put out her hand to keep him back.

"Now it's over."

"Over?" How little she knew him.

"This is the end."

"No, it is only the beginning. You were mine; I never forgot, never. They stole you from me; nothing can part us now. Nothing!"

She was in his arms again.

"It had to come, or I should have lost my reason; it's over now. Go, before he comes back."

She slipped away from him. He went out. She groped toward the door; where was it? She was blind; then she fell.

3

Martin entered his hotel; it was past twelve. The night orgy had commenced. He passed through the room thronged with dancers, his coat buttoned up to his neck, his soft hat drawn over his eyes; stood a moment looking on, a strange silent figure out of place in that decorative humanity.

He sat by the open window in his room; the noise from below was deadened by space into a soft humming sound. Waves of icy air enveloped him. He was unconscious of cold or heat. In the flash of a moment, life had taken on a different aspect; his entire being was one great pulsation. Floyd—the difficulties before him, the dishonor of it, came faintly from a distant perspective, but he thrust it fiercely behind him. The woman filled the world for him; he lived over and over that moment of tearing joy, her face transfigured with passion, her lips, her tears, the pressure of her body against his—a statue come to life, for him alone. He had been tricked out of his happiness by her mother—but now all the powers of Hell couldn't keep him away from her.

A restless night fixed his resolve. He knew exactly what he was going to do. He dressed more slowly than usual, moving about in a kind of hushed manner; he was no longer alone; she was there, clinging to him. He jumped into a taxi and drove down to Twelfth Street. The shades were lowered in the Garrison house. Next door the wreckers had been clearing away the debris; there was now a large open space where his home had been. The Italian foreman came up to him, speaking in his pleasant broken English.

"A good job, eh? Everything gone, clean as a whistle. Tomorrow we commence to build."

Martin opened the gate of the Garrison house; as he stood at the door, his hand on the knocker, he had a feeling of being mentally unstrung. Criminologists say when thieves go to commit a crime they are sustained by a strong sense of fatality, a fixed idea that it must be; they are drawn into the vortex of crime by an irresistible fascination—the lure of adventure, the justification of the equality of human rights, the spoils, the gambler's risk. Martin felt vaguely all this; a sense of excitement stimulated him, like strong liquor. He caught his breath as he entered the room he had left the night before. She was coming to him again; now he would be the first to take her in his arms, to hold her until she would consent to go with him; he would have to coax, perhaps to threaten. He set his teeth; he had decided; it must be or he would kill himself and her.

The door opened; he turned with a smile. Floyd stood there, very pale.

"Julie is not well. When I came back last night, I found her lying unconscious on the ground. Did she complain to you?"

"No."

"The doctor says it's a serious nervous collapse. They have shut me out of the room."

"Can I do anything?"

"No."

"Keep me posted, will you?"

"Yes."

He had counted with everything but that—

He waited, eating himself up with suppressed fury; grew thin, unbearable in his impatience; he would have her; nothing could prevent it but—death!

4

The telephone rang in Dr. McClaren's office. The doctor was breakfasting, but he didn't enjoy as usual his porridge with cream and heavy black bread made by his Scotch housekeeper; his mind was elsewhere. He had been up a greater part of the night with young Mrs. Garrison, who went off from one fainting spell into another; she complained of intense pains in her head. He left her sleeping under bromides; she worried him. Dr. McClaren had lived forty years in New York; a gigantic man, with bushy, iron-gray hair and eyebrows, a noble head, keen, kind eyes.

His friends had advised him to "take out his papers"; he did, and paid his taxes honestly, but never voted. He couldn't understand the political rings; he let them fight it out without help from him. Born in Edinburgh, he studied medicine at its excellent severe university, went to London to practice, starved there five years, then turned his back on an "ungrateful country" that refused an able doctor a living.

Coming over to America, he made friends with some "natives," and liked them—nice simple fellows, "they open their hearts to you, like a grab bag at a fair; everything in it is yours."

"Medicine is a paying profession among Americans; they go about with boxes of pills in every pocket."

"Doctor, my wife's just been through an operation. She's nervous, give her something to quiet her, will you?"

The doctor objected to sedatives when not absolutely necessary, but he found the frail American woman had her own chest of quieting drugs. She talked of her operation in professional terms, like a doctor. He wondered if she knew she could have no children. He wouldn't tell her; it would break her heart, poor thing. He soon found out she *did* know, and didn't break her heart about it.

With the help of his new friends, who went to unbelievable trouble and sacrifice of valuable time to show him "the ropes," he was established in the spacious home in Thirty-fourth Street, which he eventually bought; it was the only permanent thing in his life. His simple Americans became complicated millionaires. The sands of humanity shifted from decade to decade. A great city in the making left him many a time bare of patients, but the winds of immigration blew them in again. The tidal wave of Europe's overflow became a national industry—a weird wonderful gigantic machine; they put in a crazy combination of human beings, and it vomited—Americans.

The assistant put his head in the door.

"Mr. Garrison seems agitated. He would like you to come at once."

The doctor threw down his napkin and jumped into his car; the Garrisons were one of the few old families left. He was very fond of young Garrison; he had brought him into the world; nothing like that baby had even been seen before; there was a controversy about the name; Mr. Garrison wanted James, according to tradition when it had ceased to be Jan, but she wouldn't hear of anything so vulgar; she named the child Floyd, after the hero of Mrs. Holmes' last novel.

"But," said the doctor, "suppose he should develop into a strong individuality; that name would be too weak for him."

"He won't," said Prudence. "He'll be like all the men of the family, a perfect gentleman."

If Floyd's father had lived, he would never have consented to the marriage. Julie was a hysterical girl, with a tendency to epilepsy; that was a secret in a family of many secrets; she grew out of it, but there were always over developed emotional symptoms. He was called in one night. She had been taken ill at the opera; the music affected her; she was quite stiff; he brought her to with difficulty. He had a shock when he heard of Floyd's marriage. He thought there was something going on between Julie and Martin Steele. The young couple seemed to be very happy; she was a passionate mother; such mothers don't make good wives.

He stood looking down thoughtfully at the sick woman, tossing from one side of the bed to the other. He had assured Floyd it was only a nervous attack. The excavating going on in the neighborhood accounted for the chills alternating with fever. She was delirious for hours, and after, exhausted, lifeless. Floyd wanted to consult another doctor.

"No, no, not necessary yet; it would frighten the patient, but I'll send for Miss Mary."

Floyd was bewildered; Julie was in perfect health and high spirits when he left and drove with Maud to her hotel. Scarcely an hour had intervened; he found her unconscious. What did it mean?

Julie was not talkative about herself, although she drew every thought out of him. Was there anything worrying her? Could any woman have it better? He was her constant companion, anticipated her every wish; what more could he do?

He sat brooding, the breakfast before him untouched, his paper unopened. Someone was fumbling at the knocker outside; he went to the door; he had a vague impression of a very small person; a clear voice spoke; it was like a bell ringing in his ears.

"Mr. Garrison's house?"

"Yes, what can I do for you?"

"Nothing. I'm going to try to do something for you." She flew up the stairs.

He was a bit startled, as if a bird had suddenly fluttered past him. He followed her, she had already thrown off her cape, under which was a white linen dress. She took an apron and cap from her bag, quickly put them on without a mirror; they sat at just the proper angles; she was used to dressing in the dark. Julie was lying across the bed; the covering was in knots, the pillows all cavities. The girl bent over her, murmuring low sounds like a dove cooing. Floyd tried to distinguish the words.

"You're very uncomfortable. Yes, I know how your head aches. Oh, what pretty hair! It's heavy, isn't it? Let me roll it up for you. How warm you are. No wonder." She flew to the windows, let them down top and bottom, putting a screen at the bed to shield the patient from the draught.

She spoke in a low but extraordinarily clear voice, every syllable sharply cut.

"A bowl of cracked ice, please; now the linen. Don't bother; I'll find everything."

She was already in the next room exploring. When Floyd came up with ice, she was changing the sheets; it was the most remarkable feat he had ever seen, she rolled one off and slipped on the other without disturbing the patient. Her hands were tiny, but flexible, strong; it was magic. How the room changed; everything in order, the bed fresh and clean, the patient soothed. She held Julie's hand, whispering all kinds of encouraging things.

"Now I'm going to give you something to eat; you're hungry, of course you are; that husband of yours starves you."

She threw a smiling look at Floyd, who smiled back at her. She knew he spoilt his wife; he could see that.

"No, I won't go away; I'll stay right here." She took a bottle of prepared food out of her bag, which she warmed on the electric heater, cooing all the time, going about noiselessly on the smallest feet Floyd had ever seen. A trained nurse from his experience was a loud, fat, middle-aged woman who upset the house, ate all day long, and had to be waited on by the family. This little fairy was so helpful, so executive; she knew it all, she hadn't asked a question.

When Dr. McClaren came that day, he gave a quick glance around and said:

"Now everything will be all right."

Floyd followed him down stairs. After a short silence the doctor spoke.

"Has your wife any worries?"

He tried to be quite truthful.

"Oh, no; at least, none that I know of." Then he spoke about that "little girl" upstairs, remarking how wonderfully quick she was.

The doctor smiled.

"Isn't she very young?"

"She's had twenty-three years of hard experience. She was born in a hospital. Her mother died at her birth. The lot of us took care of her—the scrub woman, the nurses, the doctors, the patients; she grew up inhaling iodoform; it's healthier than eau de cologne. Her dolls were little orphan babies. She learnt to sterilize instruments at an age when most children are being 'perambulated' in the park. She toddled after me, sat on the cots, watched the patients get well, watched them die. I could have made a good doctor out of her, but she thought nursing was more helpful. Her school graduates human beings."

5

The patient improved. Miss Mary watched her drop into a quiet sleep, then flew over to see the doctor. She perched on the arm of a big chair; it wouldn't do to sit in it when one is tired; it was too comfortable—

"What are you doing here? Anything wrong?"

"No. It's that poor man."

The doctor chuckled. Floyd Garrison, spoilt child of Fortune, husband of the prettiest woman of New York's pretty women, belonging to an exclusive set, the happy father of a fine boy, and here comes this child of the gutter and calls him 'a poor man.' Ha! Ha!

"The house is going to ruin, the food spoilt; the butler steals his neckties, stockings, handkerchiefs; the cook falsifies the bills."

"Well, how can we cure that?"

"By reforming the household; would it appear obtrusive?"

"I don't know, but he's a nice fellow and you might try."

"Thanks, that's what I came for. I want to make you my partner in crime."

"Wretch." He flung a writing pad at her, which she dodged with great dexterity, and flew out.

That night the dinner was uneatable. Floyd looked helpless.

"Things are going badly, since my wife's illness."

Here was Mary's chance.

"Will you let me attend to that?"

Floyd thanked her, hoped she wouldn't bother too much, put his car at her disposal, then followed her softly up the stairs, feeling that he had managed the house very well. Julie was asleep.

"Do you think I could go to the club for a couple of hours—that is, if I'm not wanted?"

"Oh yes, go; it will do you good. Take the latch key and come in as quietly as possible."

The next morning Floyd enjoyed a good breakfast, waited on by a very pretty girl in black, with a dainty cap and apron. He had never liked a waitress—too much like a tearoom, but Ellen, the new maid, didn't give him a chance to miss the butler; she hovered around watching Miss Mary, responding to her quick glances. This amused Floyd. Martin must come to dinner; he'd fire off witticisms about being under petticoat government.

Ellen was a girl-mother; her sweetheart promised to marry her, but he didn't. Miss Mary saw her through her trouble, took her baby to Bridget, the wife of a coal heaver, who had seven babies. Mary encouraged Bridget to go on having them, but the cost of living was too high even for a coal heaver. She took the poor "bastard" to her wonderful bosom, and nursed it, happy because she didn't have to dry up her milk. Mary put Bridget in the kitchen, Ellen in the dining-room; the little brat was smuggled in, and was so quiet, Mary was sure he knew he wasn't wanted. She put a neighbor who was also "under obligations" in charge of the seven babies.

Floyd was allowed to go in every morning and sit with his wife; he noticed Mary remained in the room. He said the same thing, mechanically, every time.

"You feel better this morning, don't you?" The atmosphere of the sick room struck him dumb; that ghostly silent creature lying there wasn't Julie.

He sat at the breakfast table—well cooked, well served. There was a flutter on the stairs. Mary flew in and sat opposite him, giving him a quick glance.

"Miss Mary, we should have a night nurse."

"Oh, no, there is no necessity of another nuisance in the house."

"But, you get no sleep."

"Oh, yes, I do."

"I hear you moving about at night."

"Oh, do you? I'm sorry. I'll get a pair of soft slippers."

He went up as usual to see Julie. Mary met him at the door.

She said in a low tone:

"Just a minute and don't stay."

"You feel better this morning, don't you?"

Her eyes were very wide open; she was looking beyond him; he turned; there was nobody in the room. Miss Mary was at the telephone calling the doctor.

The sick woman raised herself in the bed, holding out her arms like a child who wants to be taken up. He bent to lift her; she pushed him away with unbelievable force.

"I don't want you. I want—Martin."

Miss Mary came flying into the room.

"What is it?" said Floyd.

"She's delirious again."

The cry never ceased; over and over again, supplicating, in a pitiable voice:

"I want Martin!"

When the doctor came, she caught at him eagerly.

"What do you want, dear lady; tell me?"

"I want Martin!"

Floyd's anguish was terrible; he was leaning against the door on the verge of a collapse. Mary signaled the doctor, who took him by the arm and led him into the next room.

"Is it Martin Steele?" said the doctor.

"Yes."

"Send for him."

"I will not. She doesn't know what she's saying." Floyd's voice was harsh. He was on his feet in a frenzy of rage.

The voice came again, louder, more despairing.

"I want Martin!"

"Do something, for God's sake!" cried Floyd.

"There is nothing to be done but wait."

The doctor went back into the room. The cry continued. Miss Mary came in.

"What is it, is she worse?"

"No, but the doctor says, 'telephone.'"

Floyd took up the receiver. What could Martin do in that room? "No! no!"

"Martin! Martin!" It came again, that cry; it was terrible.

Mary put the receiver in his hand. He called up the hotel.

The answer came, "Out."

He tried the club.

"Yes, Mr. Steele was there."

"Who is it?"

"Floyd."

"Julie?" came like a shot through the 'phone.

"She is about the same."

Floyd heard the quick gasp of relief; wonderful how a wire can bear witness.

"She has intermittent attacks of fever, calls for her grandfather, her mother; she called your name once."

"Mine?"

"It means nothing, of course, but the doctor thinks if she sees someone outside the family—"

In a short time, Martin was there. Floyd went down to meet him; neither spoke. Floyd led the way upstairs. They stopped at the door of the sick room, and heard the cry of the delirious woman.

"Martin! I want Martin!"

With a bound Martin flung himself on his knees beside the bed.

"Julie! Julie!"

She opened her eyes, heavy with fever; they wandered about, seeking! seeking!

"Julie!"

She lifted herself into his arms.

He held her close, whispering caressing words; she listened, her eyes fixed by the power of his; soon the tired lids drooped; she slept.

Martin felt the fluttering of her heart. He had no sense of time, place; the world was unpeopled; he was the only man, she the only woman. The doctor's watch registered forty minutes. Mary looked at Floyd. His eyes never left them; his wife in his friend's arms. The doctor laid the sleeping woman gently back on the pillow. Martin dropped his head down on the bed, helpless; Miss Mary led him downstairs; he fell in a heap in the chair. He was conscious now of Floyd, not the friend—a stranger, with a drawn face, an icy voice.

"What is there between you and my wife?"

The ticking of a clock became distinctly sharp. Should he tell the truth now? No; it would make it impossible for him to come again; he would wait until she got well. He put his hands on Floyd's shoulders, looking him straight in the face.

Floyd repeated his question.

"What is there between you and my wife?"

"What there has always been, a deep affection."

"You are trying to steal her from me."

"How can you think that; you told me yourself she called the names of others."

"I lied. She called no one but you."

Martin's face was telling tales; he went over to the fireplace.

"You are unjust to her, but, if you persist, I won't come again." His voice faltered; his eyes filled up. Floyd had never been able to resist him.

"You two are my only friends; if I lose you there is nobody, nobody."

He went to the door, then turned and put out his hand. They were friends again—to all appearances.

6

Mary jumped into the doctor's car, and held a consultation. She sat with her legs drawn up, her elbows on her knees, her little serious face puckered. He liked her like that; something was coming.

"Well, doctor," said he.

She put her little head on the side and returned his glance. She didn't smile as usual.

"It's a psychosis. The fever is not physical; it's a condition of the mind. I think she needs analysing."

His Scotch wrath broke over her head.

"Stop that!—I won't have it with her; this analysing has done too much mischief, dragging the wild beasts out of their caverns, showing the poor victims the horrors that are within them. I tell you, the people are playing with psycho-analysis like children with dynamite; they don't understand it, nor do we, yet. Let that woman alone, do you hear!—unless you want to rob her of the little reason she has left. She's the victim of heredity; we can't change that, can we? She's the victim of a certain physical tendency, inborn; we can't change that; she's the victim of the errors of her ancestors; we can't change that."

"No, Doctor, but we all are, if we knew it."

"It's a good thing we don't. Now I hope this woman's love for her child and her husband will counteract other influences; mind you, she's a good, innocent woman; but she is obsessed by an evil spirit which must be exorcised." There he was, the old Scotch Calvinist.

Julie was quiet until evening.

"Where is Floyd?"

"Do you want to see him?"

"Yes."

Mary flew downstairs. Floyd was trying to read the evening paper; trying to be just to his wife, his friend. He hated to be suspicious; it turned the honey of life to gall; such thoughts made him ill; he couldn't live with them. He heard a patter, patter. Mary put her head in the door, beckoning him. He found Julie crushed into the pillows.

"Miss Mary says I've been out of my head."

Floyd was vexed. Why did Miss Mary tell her that?

"Did I say irrational things?"

"No, just babbled a bit."

"What did I say?"

"Only disconnected words without meaning."

She evidently didn't know what had happened.

Floyd smoked his pipe that night, and read Emerson on Friendship. Martin was to be pitied; he was a lonely wretch; he'd give him the benefit of the doubt. Mary came in to say good night.

"Everything is all right. We'll close up early. She'll have a quiet night, I hope."

The hope was not realized. The sick woman had a terrible night; her pulse was jumping like a frenzied thing, but her mind was clear. She clung frantically to Mary.

"I'm lost! save me! save me!" then she broke into convulsive sobbing, always begging to be helped. Mary shut the door carefully. It wouldn't do for that "poor man" to hear.

Floyd tossed uneasily. He was sure there was something mentally wrong with Julie; he had heard of women getting "queer" after weaning a child. He had been too harsh with Martin. She had called him in her delirium; that meant nothing. Martin had wanted to marry her, but it was all long forgotten; she was *his* wife now, the mother of his child; it was foolish to make a fuss about a few moments of delirium. Julie would never know about it.

"What was that?"

He jumped out of bed and listened. He thought he heard somebody calling, "Martin! Martin!"

Julie's door was shut; all was still. It was his own imagination; that cry was still in his ears. He went back to bed; he must get that idea out of his head; he wouldn't let it become a mania with him. He would see Martin often, have him to dinner. It was low of him to keep on thinking evil of them both. The thought acted like a sedative; he slept.

He was up and dressed before seven. The night's depression descended again over him like a black veil. There was a knock; Mary stood outside, pale, agitated.

"What is it? What is it?"

"Come and see."

It was dark. He saw Julie's figure lying across the bed; she was in a deep sleep. Mary opened a shutter gently. He stifled an exclamation. The long thick wavy hair flowing loosely over the pillow, over her heart, had turned white; she lay in an ocean of foam. What had happened to her in the night? What had been at work in her brain?—he had heard vaguely of a sudden shock turning the hair white. He gazed and gazed; it was as if an artist had dipped his brush into molten silver and drawn it through every hair in her head. Another long look; then he went downstairs, putting his hand on the balustrade to support himself.

Mary closed the shutter softly and followed him. His mind was confused. The ordeal with his wife, culminating in this, was too much; he needed help. She waited, standing quietly beside him. He felt her intense sympathy; then he said in a low, hushed voice:

"What could have caused it?"

"It can easily be accounted for. Your wife is subject to violent nervous headaches; she had an attack in the night."

"Was she sobbing?"

"Yes, she suffered terribly. We must be brave for her sake."

He looked at her standing there, her eyes shining, undaunted, courageous. Where did she get that spirit? She was no longer only a nurse; she was a comrade, a fellow-fighter; her voice was like a call to arms.

"I was always very happy," he said. "I mean, I thought it was happiness, but I see now that it was like being under shelter when others were destitute; that kind of happiness is selfish, isn't it?"

"Yes," said Mary. "That's why I try not to be too happy."

"My parents were my only friends. They left me; I had only my wife. Perhaps I wanted too much from her; she was unfortunate in her family; I should have taken better care—I—can't see ahead! I don't know how this will affect her. I—I don't know."

"It will be a blow, but you can soften it for her."

"I, what can I do?"

Mary hesitated. Why was she obliged to say what he should have known intuitively: did he love his wife?

"Her heart would be at rest if you would convince her it doesn't matter to you what color her hair is."

He was on his feet, his eyes averted.

"You want me to tell her?"

"Yes."

He went to the door, then came back. "Will you come with me?"

"It's better for you to go alone."

He entered his wife's room, sat down beside the bed, feeling like an intruder. She awoke startled, her eyes were deep with the sleep-shadows of opiates.

"Did I frighten you?"

"No, but I felt someone was here—Something has happened! Tell me?"

"Yes. Your hair."

"What about my hair?"

"It has turned gray since last night." She was out of bed with a bound, standing before the mirror.

"Let in the light."

He went from window to window; the sun struck the surface of the looking glass, dancing in and out of the silver veil that enveloped her.

She gave a low cry, and shrunk away.

"Julie, don't grieve about what can't be helped; it often happens from such headaches; it's your nerves." He wanted to say, "You will always be the same to me because I love you." He couldn't.

"It is not a symptom, it is a punishment."

"You have done nothing to deserve punishment."

She looked at him, through him, past him. He didn't know her thoughts; that door was closed to him.

"I want to see Miss Mary."

Mary was surprised to find her patient sitting up in bed. She had wound her hair in a tight coil around her head, covering it with a heavy lace cap.

"Miss Mary, I am feeling better this morning; I don't think I shall need you any longer."

Mary gasped. Where was the exhausted creature of the night before, the helpless invalid?

"I'm very glad, Mrs. Garrison. Any time you send for me, I will come." Then she took Julie's hand, bent forward and kissed her; there was a slight quiver of the mouth.

"Don't think I'm ungrateful, but I couldn't bear you to say anything; it's unspeakable, good-bye."

Floyd was waiting in the hall when Mary came down with her hat on, carrying her suitcase.

"You are not going?"

"There is nothing more for me to do here. Your wife is better; the shock will cure her." Then she smiled at him. "I'm aching for the slums; my cradle stood there; there I learnt what life means; when I get thinking too much of myself, I go back and learn again."

He went with her to the door, and held her hand in a strong grasp; he could think of nothing worth saying. A cloud of dust blew in their faces; they were pulling down the little row of brick houses on the other side.

Floyd stopped in the hall to brush himself off. The wreckers were working within him, scattering debris. He went up to his wife's room again, listened; there was no sound. He turned the knob cautiously; the door was locked. There was a sense of relief; he wouldn't have to spend the morning in that dark room. He jumped into a taxi and drove to his club.

7

Julie gradually recovered; there was a feeling of strength in her limbs, a desire for movement she hadn't felt since the birth of her child; it was the strength of despair. One day she took out her pretty gowns and hung them one by one on silk hangers in the room next to her bedroom. It had been Floyd's den; he used to sit there at night during the first year of their marriage, reading. He could see his darling in her lace-trimmed bed. She complained she had no place to hang the Paris creations he bought for her; he suggested putting racks around his den, which they did; those lace, gold and silver gowns seemed to him to hang on bodies which swayed to and fro in the draught. The face was always Julie's, in her different moods. The perfume stifled him. He had an old-fashioned idea about perfume; his mother never used it. He gave up reading there at night.

She put her hats in boxes, her slippers, stockings, lingerie, wrapped carefully in tissue paper, in an old bureau, a family relic which Floyd refused to sell; it was two hours of fatiguing work, but she wasn't tired. She opened the door and peered out; there was no one about; she crept down the stairs, went from room to room, covered furniture and mirrors with gray linen, and crept up again. When Ellen came home with the boy, she noticed her dark shining hair. She dismissed her on the spot, and rang up for the Japanese butler to come back.

Floyd was shocked to find the house so bare and cheerless.

"Why have you had the covers put on again?"

"It's dusty. The furniture will be ruined, and we're not going to entertain."

He didn't answer. When he saw the Japanese, he asked for Ellen.

"Oh! I sent her away."

"Why! has she done anything wrong?"

"No! but she annoys me, she's too good-looking."

Floyd feared his wife's mind was unbalanced; she brooded too much over her misfortune. He was very tender, very indulgent, but sometimes his patience gave out.

Days, weeks, months passed. Winter came with snow, ice, sleet. Julie spent most of the time in her room, rarely going down to dinner. Floyd tried to get her out for a walk, but had to compromise with the automobile. She'd wear a hat pulled down over her eyes, a thick veil, a long close-fitting coat, and avoided Fifth Avenue. The house remained covered. Floyd begged her to take off those ugly, depressing gray things, but she sat silent, antagonistic; it always ended in his dashing out, and spending the day at the club. But his anger never lasted. The pathetic figure, crouching in a big chair, those weary lustreless eyes, hurt him terribly; she had lost her beauty. What is the elusive thing we call beauty? It is not form, it is not color; it is something that pervades, like the perfume of a flower in fresh earth, or a haunting magic in the woods. In a woman it is a living spark that sets us aglow; that spark was dead in Julie; he had to admit it. The Image which he called by her name was blurred; she would be an old, miserable woman; he, an old, disappointed man.

He spent much of his time at the club. He'd read his morning paper there. He detested local politics. The society column annoyed him; Mrs. C. had run off with her chauffeur, Mrs. M. was going to marry her riding master, a well-known woman was suing her millionaire husband for more alimony. It was horrible to have one's domestic horrors made attractive reading; he resolved no one should suspect his. Then the paper would drop from his hand, the green Park grow shadowy, fade away; he'd awaken with a sense of guilt; a young man dozing in his chair, and all the unrest in the world. He would look about furtively; the others didn't notice—they too were dozing.

One day he went home earlier than usual. Julie, with the boy in her arms, was sitting at the window watching the workingmen on the iron frame of a building opposite; they were knocking, boring, climbing in and out like monkeys; it was fascinating. She was conscious of her flannel wrapper. Floyd was always well dressed, well groomed; his glance was like a sharp whip. He took the boy from her and put him on the bed.

"The child is heavy, you must not accustom him to be carried about; he makes the house unbearable with his cries. It's all right to be a good mother, but you are overdoing it; you forget you have a husband."

She was on her feet facing him indignantly.

"How can you speak to me like that? You have no pity for my misfortune!"

"I'm sorry if I have offended you, but I don't see why you should be so sensitive about your hair. You have become very neglectful; you have lost all self-respect. I'm ashamed of the servants."

"Floyd!"

"I want to have Colonel Garland for dinner; I have business with him."

"No, no; I won't see him."

"Very well. It's not very pleasant for a married man to be obliged to invite his friends to a restaurant, because his wife will not take the trouble to make herself presentable."

"The dinner will be served whenever you order it, but I will not come down."

"You can do as you please about that. I'll ask him for Wednesday."

"Not so soon?" She was panic-stricken.

"My mother never needed to prepare. Her table was always well supplied."

With this parting shot he went out.

Julie stood aghast; her adoring slave was turning against her. A man loves only beauty in a woman; when she loses that, she loses everything. She was so young; what was she going to do with the rest of her life? She sat despairing, trying to think herself out of the network of misery which entangled her. She couldn't, poor thing. The present was a horror to her; the future, a blank. She went back to the past, lived it all over again and again— Martin! the joy of those secret meetings; Hippolyte—the side-door which opened only wide enough to slip into the dark corridor; there, in Martin's arms——

The child cried; she threw herself down beside him, pressing him violently to her. He struggled. She held him tightly—muttering unconsciously, "My body, my Soul, my little Martin," peering into his face—as if seeking something to console her. These paroxysms of despair sapped her strength. She was no longer apathetic, but groping, groping for some remedy. She'd go back always to those wonderful days with Martin. She was religious at heart, but she would have gladly given her hopes of redemption to be able to look into the mirror and see once more her young face, her soft dark hair. Hippolyte had admired her hair; she saw him again, so suave, so handsome, heard his exquisite French, caught again the laughing significance of the looks which passed between the two men—It was madly fascinating; day and night it all repeated itself in her brain, revolving like an ever-turning wheel— Martin—Hippolyte—Pierrot—the sweet, pungent odor of the place; then the suggestion worked. Hippolyte had often told them of his wonderful salves, lotions, hair restorers—he might know a way to restore the color of her hair. She looked up his address—took the receiver in her hand, a moment of fear, irresolution, then she called the number.

"I want to speak to Hippolyte."

"Oui, Madame, I am here."

His voice set her nerves quivering.

"It's Mrs. Garrison speaking. You don't know my married name, I was Julie Gonzola."

"Madame, I knew your voice. How could I forget it?"

"Will you come and see me today at four? Thank you."

She was terribly excited. What would he think when he saw her now? He must help her—he must! It was her last hope.

Punctually at four, the boy knocked.

"A gentleman downstairs."

She shrunk away—she couldn't see him.

"He says you expect him."

With a strong effort she controlled the impulse to send the man away.

"Show him up."

Hippolyte looked curiously at Julie, not grasping what had happened to her. She was embarrassed, didn't know what to say; then she slipped off her cap and let her hair down. It fell to the bottom of her dress. He gasped and broke into a shower of compliments. His admiration was evidently sincere. Julie's spirits rose; it was not all over.

"My hair turned white when I was ill. I want it restored to its natural color; I can give you the shade—"

"*Mais non! Madame*, it is quite *le dernier cri*—we are bleaching the hair now, but we couldn't do it like this, Madame. Your hair will be the sensation; it needs a little tonic oil and massage." Then he looked at her again. "Madame is long indisposed?"

"Yes, I have been in the house all winter."

"Madame needs fresh air and the Swedish treatment—the beauty will come back; put yourself in my hands, and you will see!"

8

The Wednesday agreed on, arrived. Floyd left the house without seeing Julie; he was getting used to that; the entire morning she would be occupied with the boy, always in a wrapper with that disfiguring cap on her. She bathed, dressed, undressed the child like a professional nurse. Floyd protested in vain.

On the way downtown he telephoned the house.

"Is Madame awake yet?"

"Oh, yes, sir."

"Connect me with her room, will you?"

Julie called "Hello." He thought her voice had more life in it than usual.

"Julie, do you remember I was to ask Colonel Garland to dinner tonight, but if you are still against it, I can postpone it."

"Oh, no! The dinner is ordered."

"Thank you."

He dropped the receiver with a guilty feeling. Perhaps he had been too harsh. He didn't know what to do about her; he was quite helpless; life was becoming unbearable.

Colonel Garland greeted Floyd with delight. He was talking to a tall man in his private office who came up and shook hands.

"You don't remember me, Mr. Garrison?"

Floyd took in the tired face, the dark-rimmed eyes, the deep lines.

"Yes, I do! Are you still 'sweating blood' for money?"

"No, I'm sweating blood to keep it."

"Have you any left?"

"A few drops, but I'll be bled white if this goes on."

He laughed mirthlessly, said "So-long," and left.

The Colonel looked after him, speaking with a touch of pity and contempt.

"That fellow made a million during the War; it's been going the other way for some time, and—he's got a handsome, extravagant wife. Now—if we pull down those old shanties near the river, and build up big warehouses—"

"No! no! I'm not a wrecker; they bring enough for my modest wants."

"That's just what your father said twenty years ago. You're getting very much like him."

Floyd didn't take that as a compliment. The men of twenty years ago were a century behind the times. Then, rather timidly, hoping for a refusal, he said:

"Will you come and take pot-luck with me tonight? My wife's not well; she can't join us—I must find some congenial occupation. We'll talk it over."

The Colonel was all animation.

"Politics! We need young men. We've got a job on our hands to rebuild the world."

Late in the afternoon they went to the Republican Club for a cocktail from the Colonel's private stock. There were the usual jokes about Prohibition being a good law—for others. On alighting from the car, Floyd was surprised to see the soft red gleam of the colored glass fixture over the porch. The filmy lace window curtains through which the light shone were not there when he left the house that morning; before he could take out his latch key, the door was swung open. The Jap in spotless white smiled a welcome; they entered the parlor—

"By God," cried the Colonel, "this is something like. A beautiful color, that velvet."

Floyd smiled. "Mulberry, they call it."

The chairs, the sofa with its cushions, were like old friends; he saw again those well-loved water colors; his mother looking down at him, and through the door, the glimpse of a beautifully set dinner table—a picture covered for a long time, once more in the light.

Julie came swiftly toward them, extending her hand to the Colonel. She was in a state of excitement, like an actress who makes her début in a new rôle. Her color came and went. A crescent of black plaster deepened the darkness of her eyes. The despised hair revenged itself with its beauty; it was mounted in shining, rippling masses on the top of her head. She wore a soft white gown, embroidered with seed pearls, a train of gold sweeping the ground. Her arms and neck were free of ornament; in her corsage a large red American Beauty rose. At dinner she kept up a flow of small talk accentuated by soft glances, winning smiles. The Colonel listened as if every word were a new truth, the usual platitudes taking on a mysterious significance. He was sixty, held himself very erect, could easily be taken for ten years younger, and he loved the ladies.

Floyd was silent, trying to overcome a queer feeling. Was this gracious, smiling woman his wife? Was he sitting at his own table? Who was he, anyhow? The Colonel's stentorian voice with its agreeable Southern accent broke in on his confused mental condition.

"If you will permit me to tell you how much I admire your perfect taste in dress. You know what suits you—an inspiration to powder your hair."

"Oh," laughed Julie, "it's not powdered, it's natural. It runs in our family to turn gray early. My father was white at twenty-one."

The gallant Colonel turned this to his credit.

"My dear Mistress Garrison, Nature has been your Fairy Godmother; she has waved her wand over your head, bestowing one charm more, the gift of original beauty."

The evening passed quickly in light persiflage, Floyd listening as if he were in the auditorium of a theatre. At the door the Colonel gave one look back. He could have fought a duel for her.

"We haven't had a chance to talk business," said Floyd.

"Who could, with such a radiant vision before us?" laughed the Colonel. "Come down to the office."

Floyd went back to Julie.

"Thank you for making such a sacrifice." It sounded foolish, but he didn't know what to say.

She came closer to him. He was afraid to touch her; she was like a strange woman in his house. That soft sensual smile set him on fire. She slid into his arms; he kissed her neck, hair, her lips; she let herself be adored. His love had been ideal in those early wonderful days of his marriage. He reverenced his wife; he was afraid to repel her. He had heard of some men whose wives hated them for their lack of consideration. Julie laughed at his innocence. He often wondered if she appreciated being his first love; he couldn't answer that now, after four years. He ceased trying to probe her soul; he worshipped her body.

In the physical intoxication of the next few months, he forgot all his plans for future activity. Love can be a despot or a liberator; Floyd was in chains again.

9

When it was known the Garrisons had "come back," they were deluged with invitations.

"Do you want to go?"

"Of course, what's the use of Paris gowns if I can't make the other women green?" She was in good humor now, caressed, spoilt, every wish fulfilled. He gave her a new car, a gorgeous thing fitted up like a boudoir, trying to shake off a sickening consciousness that he was buying her favors. He pulled wires for a box at the opera (it was an achievement to get one); she rewarded him with a long kiss; he developed a prodigality which astounded the Colonel.

"You're going it, my boy. You're beyond your income."

"Oh, sell something," laughed Floyd. "I must have money."

The Colonel didn't like the flippant answer, the restless way. He wasn't quite certain, but it seemed once or twice the boy had been drinking. He had noticed since Prohibition many sober men had taken to drink; psychologically interesting, the resistance to personal restraint....

The opening night of the opera, Julie was the centre of attraction. She had taken the family jewels out of the safe deposit. A great cluster of diamonds set in antique silver shone on her velvet bodice of old wine, a glittering aigrette in her hair which was no longer an old gray—treatment had changed it into the mat silver which one sees on the head of a marble statue, with life added to its charm. She stood in the box in her velvet wrap; Floyd took it off with a feeling of excitement. He felt the sensation she created; he was running a blooded mare for the first prize.

Maud sat in front with Tom Dillon. She had played her last trump in the game of matrimony. It wasn't a King now, but a Knave who cared for her;

she was sure of that. For the rest, she looked into her mirror and saw her future; it spelt wrinkles.

"Who is that gorgeous creature?"

"Don't you know your friend Julie Garrison?" She put up her lorgnette.

"What has she done with her hair?"

"Bleached it. Catch up, Maudy. A celebrated cocotte in Paris has made white hair the rage; she looks like one, doesn't she?"

"Yes, she does—wonderful. I always said Julie had great possibilities; there's something about her that attracts men. Look at Martin."

He was standing against a post opposite the box. His eyes fastened on Julie, his mouth twisted into a derisive smile; the Colonel was there pouring out his usual compliments. Men were coming in and out, old club friends of Floyd's, all eager to renew their acquaintance. Julie's illness had upset all his calculations, but there was one cause for satisfaction: she had wanted *him*, *he* had saved her, she belonged to *him*, not Floyd. He was waiting for a propitious moment; she must tell Floyd the truth. He waited because he was not sure of her; after a long siege of fever, the blood cools off.

He dropped in one day at Hippolyte's Parlor—he went there now to hear about Julie. "Madame was going to have a dinner party,"—he had made a supreme effort. The phenomenon of her hair had given him a great deal of thought. He was in his way a scientist; the psychic side of it interested him. "You must see her superb hair; it suits her to perfection. It gives the last touch of that '*Je ne sais quoi*' which she lacked. It was caused in my opinion by some intense subconscious passion." Martin bent over eagerly. "A psychic power which acts like the eruption of a volcano; it tears her, agonizes her, she struggles with it, is not quite able to translate it—yet— Her husband is a nice fellow, *mais vous savez*, Puritanism, the narrow path; he'll never deceive her, nor pardon her if she deceives him. That little house is no frame for a woman like her. She needs life, sparkle, passion—*Voila tout!*"

During the next few months Hippolyte's mademoiselle brought now and again a deep red rose, and set it in an exquisite glass vase on Julie's dressing table. Julie asked no questions; her eyes glistened. She furtively put the rose to her lips; then she'd sit for hours under the hands of the French woman, massage, electric treatment, hot—cold, until her body exhaled an indefinable intoxicating perfume....

Maud and Tom made their way to the Garrison box. Julie, with a keen woman's look, saw at once that Maud's gown, jewelry, furs, were no longer imitations. Tom was evidently embarrassed and hung back. Floyd rather liked him; he was genuine; he didn't disguise the fact that he was a rotter. He said, "I'm no good; take me as I am, or not at all."

"What have you been doing all this time?"

"Oh! nothing much," laughed Maud, "shopping, house hunting, getting married; we didn't announce it, it wasn't worth while." Floyd grasped Tom's hand.

"I couldn't get her, any other way, so we called on the Judge—We've been married six weeks; so far it's all right—I'm going to buy a house and put it in her name—If I don't behave myself, she can kick me out."

Maud was sitting in front with Julie, talking over joining the young matrons and giving a series of dinners.

Suddenly she said:

"Have you seen Martin Steele lately?"

"I've been ill a long time."

"He's here tonight."

"Yes, I saw him standing at the back."

"He looks awful, doesn't he?"

Julie didn't answer. Maud said afterwards to her husband: "Julie was always different from the rest of us; she was queer tonight, didn't hear a word I said. I'm certain she's not all there."

As they were going out, they passed Martin.

"Come with us to the dancing club. Tom's sure to take too much; you can help me get him home."

Martin went, but it was Tom who had to take Martin home, abusingly drunk, fighting like a beast.

That night Julie had dreams, and talked in her sleep. She flung her arms around Floyd.

"I'm so glad you love me just the same." Floyd was a happy man. He had finished his breakfast and was looking out of the front window, waiting for his wife to awaken.

"Floyd, Floyd."

He went up the stairs three at a time.

She held out her arms to him.

"Floyd, we must move away from here; the street is getting impossible." A crash of falling timbers next door strengthened her position.

"Julie! This is our home; you know how I love it. How can you ask me such a thing?"

He was losing his temper; she was on the verge of tears, and last night when he held her in his arms, he swore—they all do at those times.

"I'll do anything for you, anything, but my home is a part of me; you don't realize how I love it."

"More than me?" She was pouting now, like a child.

"Oh, no!—different—you won't ask me to leave it, will you?" It was pathetic, the appeal in the man's voice.

"But I also loved my home; I left it for you."

He was about to say, "It's not the same. The roots of my life are here; you are an alien." He didn't want to offend her; then he went down to see the Colonel, and mentioned with much embarrassment that the street was getting unbearable.

"Yes, it's very unhealthy for your wife and child to inhale all that dust. We've secured a house."

"Oh, have you? My wife didn't tell me."

"No, she wanted to give you an agreeable surprise. It's on Park Avenue. We've rented it for the winter." He didn't add, with the privilege of buying; that was to be kept secret. He liked to be in conspiracy with Julie against her husband.

"It's perfection; we've secured it with servants, wine cellar, everything complete."

Floyd went home and compromised with Julie. The furnished house for the winter only; he was grateful she had not insisted on going to a fashionable hotel!—A camp in the mountains for the summer, and in the autumn when the street was built up, to return to the old home. Julie was satisfied with the bargain. The house would be impossible shut in on both sides; the walls were cracking; everything was going to pieces. She would never go back.

Floyd stood at the door of the car waiting for the "bunch" to come down— the boy, the nurse, the Pekinese, countless bags, dress suit cases, last-minute bundles, and—Julie very much excited. She had gone back for the little glass vase which had been forgotten. He was physically tired, mentally agonized; he cast one look back and jumped into the car. He had a peculiar feeling: he was the automobile; Julie was driving.

The house in Park Avenue was the very last word; Floyd had to confess that. The walls tinted a cold gray, the light coming from invisible corners, telephones, a radio-cabinet, china closets hidden behind panels; the entire floor could be made into a dancing hall by pushing the doors into the wall; no fireplace, very little furniture, meals rolled in ready to serve by the "haughty" Swede hired with the house, everything cooked "à la mode" by a chef, also hired with the house.

Julie was hysterical with joy; she had been all her life the victim of antiques; this was all so exquisitely modern. Floyd thought with intense longing of his little home; he vowed to himself he would not desert it; he'd go there every day and read his evening paper.

The house-warming was to be a brilliant affair. Maud with her restless activity schemed various plans for a sensational success. Tom sampled the cellar; it was perfection. Floyd was dispatched here, there, and everywhere; Julie sat back and gave the others carte blanche.

"Don't consult me," she said; "you three will do it all right."

On the day of the dinner, Julie had been the entire afternoon in the hands of Hippolyte's skilled lieutenants. He himself was to come later and give her hair the last touches.

True to his resolve, Floyd had spent his afternoons in the little house, reading his paper; but he was beginning to feel a superstitious dread when he put the key in the door. That day the room seemed unbearably chilly; he lit the fire with great difficulty. The wood piled up in a basket was damp, it sputtered awhile, gave out sighs as if it were in pain. Soon the fretful flame died out. He couldn't read, looked at his watch, and went home.

The perfume from his wife's room pervaded the house. His room was on the floor above—they had become fashionable. He saw less and less of Julie, she had no time for him; she was wrapped up in herself, her looks, her gowns; vanity had developed in her to such an extent it staggered him; she sought admiration, was a slave to style, adopting the daily change no matter how extreme; a night at home was unbearable to her; he dragged himself along; he wasn't jealous of the crowd of men always around her; but it wouldn't look well for the husband to be absent.

He hadn't seen Martin for a very long time. He was sure Julie had forgotten him, she couldn't love anyone but herself; he pulled himself up; he mustn't think that way. He remembered her as a girl, so yielding, so sweet. Illness changes the character of people sometimes. He must be patient with her; but life had become very hard; the nights were spent in carousing. He didn't know what to do with his days until Julie woke up—and he was only thirty.

He dressed and went down to his wife's door—his Mecca; it was open. Hippolyte, with a strand of her hair over his shoulder, was bending down talking confidentially. Floyd abominated him; a man who could make a fortune out of the vanity of women was despicable; but most fortunes are directly or indirectly made out of the vanity of women.

"Floyd, come in, I've such news for you. I've sold our house."

"What house?"

"Our little house, to Hippolyte."

"You're mad."

Julie gave him a quick surprised look, and got rid of Hippolyte.

"Floyd, you shouldn't speak to me like that before Hippolyte; he'll tell the next customer we quarrel." There was a suspicion of tears.

"Julie! you're mad! quite mad! What the devil can he do with our house?"

"He'll make a fortune out of it, if he follows my advice; the first floor will be a fine Colonial tea room; the old furniture and our kitchen coppers will be just the thing; the second floor, a beauty parlor; and above, in your father's workshop, a Turkish bath."

And she could sit there calmly and say such things.

The Colonel came in early, poured out a volley of compliments which put her in good humor. She whispered to him.

"I've won; he's getting used to it."

The dinner was delayed until past ten, waiting for Maud and Tom who arrived with profuse apologies. Tom had been running all day from one shop to another trying to find a string of beads for Maud.

"Costly things, those glass beads," said Tom. "Reminds me of the squaws up in the Reservation, when I was travelling with whiskey; they had them around the waist, neck, legs, through the ears and nose, and by God! they thought they were in full dress."

When the dancing commenced, Julie was surrounded; she was the prettiest woman in the room, and a wonderful dancer. Floyd, in the next room among some loose fellows, was drinking heavily. The sedans were *not* ordered back; chauffeurs gossip among themselves, and after twelve, the guests were going "slumming." Taxis were engaged—Masks and dominos were put on in the hall, one not knowing who the other was; Maud had done the pairing—she saw to it that husband and wife did not meet. Tom was to have Julie, Maud selected Floyd; *he* wouldn't make love to her.

The masked figures in dominos slipped past the sentinel at the door; he was the devil who was sending souls to Hell that night.

Floyd wanted to fight everybody, then broke down and blubbered; Tom had a fellow feeling, put him in a chair, and told the haughty Swede to look after him. At the door he got mixed up in the crowd, found himself with someone in a taxi. A pair of soft lips met his, he shouted for joy.

"Maudy! where's Julie?"

She laughed. "Oh, she's in very good company." She nestled up to him. "Don't think of her, only ourselves. Let's make believe we're not married."

The taxis were speeding downtown. Julie took off her mask, leaned back; she was excited, warm from dancing. Her companion bent over her. She looked into flaming eyes.

"Julie!"

That hour in Martin's arms, she forgot her husband, her child, herself; promised him everything. This time, he swore, she should keep her word.

11

Floyd had an insane desire to smash things. He threw a bottle of wine into the glass and china on the table, overturning the electric candles; the fuse burnt out, putting the room in darkness. He laughed hysterically. He was on a ship, in a terrible storm, the ground was slipping away, billows were rising on all sides.

"Hey there, steward, damn it, where's my cabin?"

The haughty Swede lifted him like a child, carried him into the elevator which took them up to the servants' quarters, unlocked a small door at the extreme end of the hall; it was an unused room, with one lamp hanging from the ceiling. He put Floyd on the sofa, lit the lamp, and carefully shut the door—he didn't want the "master's" ravings to be heard. The caterer's men were still in the house. Some might inform; a raid would lose him his place.

When Floyd awoke, the lamp sputtered in fitful gleams. His head was like lead, his tongue parched; there was a sense of deep humiliation, waves of shame, higher than the ocean. He looked about the room. It was in disorder—boxes piled up in a corner, a large desk strewn with papers; at the door stood the Swede.

"Where am I? Whose room is this?"

"This is a room we keep closed, sir."

"Why?"

"The master killed himself here, the mistress locked the door and gave me the key; she ordered me not to open it until she came again. She didn't come."

"Where is she?"

"In Paris, sir."

"He killed himself and she went to Paris?"

"Yes sir, shot himself. He was a fine man, sir, a very fine man. When I came in to announce dinner, he was lying on that sofa where you are, the blood pouring out."

Floyd was on his feet, quite sober now. There were heavy dark stains on the gray rep. The man answered Floyd's questioning look.

"That's blood, sir, and this and this." The gray rug was stained in dark red; there were splashes of it on the white wall.

"Why did you put me in here?"

"Because the house was full of strange people. I didn't want them to see you like that."

"Thank you, I'm much obliged to you."

"Shall I bring you a little whiskey and soda?"

"No thank you, I'm not a drinker."

"I see that, sir," said the man. "A cup of strong black coffee will set you all right."

"Thank you."

Floyd looked about the room. On the desk there was a box half filled with cigars, stationery, postage stamps, everything just as the unhappy man had left them. The Swede came in with some strong black coffee which Floyd swallowed.

"Colonel Garland told me to give you this when you came to." It was a large legal envelope; Floyd took it mechanically, flung it on the desk.

"When you are ready, sir, I'll lock up here."

Floyd stood fascinated. It was the only room in that big house that meant something more than wood—marble—The desk was littered, the pigeon-holes stuffed with papers, the deep armchairs, the heavy draperies belonged to former days, the man must have had trouble with his wife about it; she had put him and his "old sticks" in the garret.

The legal envelope was lying on the desk where he had thrown it. He took out a typewritten document. The little house was in his wife's name. The Colonel had suggested it as a wedding gift. "It was only a matter of form, it was the custom for a man to put the home in the wife's name," Floyd laughingly assented. What did it matter? All he had was hers, himself included. Here it was in black and white, sold on easy terms to Hippolyte; at the bottom was written in her large clear hand, Julie Abravanel Gonzola Garrison; she had done it without consulting him; she had the right.

The monotonous voice of the Swede broke the silence.

"He was a very fine man, sir—and a liberal man. She was a beauty; that's her picture."

On the desk was a colored print of a woman in bridal costume, all lace, satin-orange blossoms, an enormous bouquet half hiding her face; it was like the wax models one sees in a show window.

The Swede took a photo out of his pocket and handed it to Floyd.

"This is the master; I asked him for it the night before he died. I was very fond of him," his voice broke.

Floyd knew that care-lined face: "The man who sweated blood." He shivered. He tried to pull himself together; the horror of it struck him down. He staggered against the desk; on it lay an open letter, crushed together, as if thrown there in haste; his eye caught unconsciously what was written.

It's over. I've made superhuman efforts; everything is gone. I was afraid to tell you the last time you demanded money, throwing up to me I hadn't made good. I told you this house would ruin us, but you didn't care! What's the good of a man who can't pay out? I've begged and begged; this is the last time! You said you couldn't be poor, and there are others. That's always in my ears! I see now what a fool I've been! I've spent my best years scheming for money, and you took it and flung it in the air. I've had nothing from my life! nothing! It's too late to commence again. Come back! Come back!

Floyd shuddered. He looked again at the blood stains; he saw the man with a pistol in his hand. It wasn't a fair exchange—his soul for her body. He sat in the big chair; that other man must have crouched there with the pistol in his hand. He had usurped a sanctuary, bought with money what another had built with blood.

"I'm ready to lock up the room, sir."

He staggered to his feet, thrust the legal envelope in his pocket, went downstairs and into the street.

The sedans rolled up and down the avenue. People stepped out in front of brilliantly lit residences, a happy care-free crowd, or were they like him, a lie?

He moved mechanically, elbowing his way through the mass of theatre-goers, gradually getting down into the business district, quiet, dark. He stood before his old home, huddled together as if shrinking away from the giant buildings on either side, unlocked the door; there was an odor like a crypt. He struck a match, lit the half-burnt candle on the hall stand, held it high, peering into the corners, through open doors, taking in every well-known detail—the straight-back mahogany chairs covered with mulberry velvet, the "tidies." He could see the shuttle in his mother's delicate fingers dancing in and out of the white thread—the rag rugs made by his grandmother. People were hunting for them in little country villages; antiquarians were reproducing them by thousands; but these were *his* rags. He went slowly up the narrow stairs; the creaking of the boards used to anger him when his mother was ill. He looked out at the desolate garden through little glass panes, just large enough for a boy's face. He saw himself again gloating over the first snow-storm, running down to the cellar for his sled, his feet dancing impatiently whilst Prudence tied the soft warm shawl she had knitted for him about his head and neck.

He stopped at the first landing. The old clock was covered with dust; he found the key inside, wound it, set it right; its ticking echoed through the house; it seemed to him like a human thing whose heart had stopped for fright, then commenced to beat again in glad relief. He opened the door of the bedroom. Here he had brought his bride, here his boy was born, here he had watched Martin holding his wife in his arms. On the dressing-table was a faded rose; it fell to pieces in his hand. He went up to his father's workshop; the images took on life in the flicker of the candle light—the Negro, the Italian shoe boy, his mother clasping him in her arms, an unfinished bust of his father, Rip Van Winkle with his head smashed—he took it all in; a life picture, the background stretching out in the full sunlight of generations, an old landscape. He was framed in it—he himself—that self, simple, sentimental, ideal, old-fashioned—the self that was not cynical, reckless, material, and all the things we call "modern." He scented the smell of fallen plaster, felt the shaking of timbers; the wreckers had him under the hammer, destroying his foundations.

The table was littered with old newspapers and rags used in modelling; he stood for a moment motionless, like a man offering a sacrifice on the altar of his domestic gods, then he dropped the candle. Little flames started here, there, grew bigger; the illumination cast a glow over his mother's face. She smiled at him. He shut the door, groping his way downstairs; at the gate he stopped to listen to the clear chime of the clock as it struck one, two, three....

There was no trace of the night orgy in the Park Avenue mansion. He went up to his wife's room; she was in bed sleeping quietly. The soft-shaded lamp which burnt through the night—she had a horror of darkness—cast a soft rosy glow. "Was this beautiful creature lying there, his wife? No! No!—a legalized mistress, and he, a sensualist."

In that moment passion burnt up in him—the body of love, the Idol, fell in ashes. He took the bill of sale from his pocket, put it beside her on the bed, then went slowly up to his room, shut the door, and burst into a loud laugh.

12

The next morning at breakfast he read the press headings.

"The old Garrison homestead destroyed by fire, a total loss, on account of Mr. Garrison's neglect to renew the insurance. Fire caused by a cigarette or cigar stump thrown carelessly from one of the tall adjacent buildings. The house was a tinder box. Fortunately, the family had moved to their palatial residence on Park Avenue."

He marked the notices with red pencil, and sent them up on his wife's breakfast tray. He heard the maid knocking, and Julie's voice saying "Come in." He could see her opening the papers, reading the marked lines; there was a loud cry and a heavy fall; he went up quickly. She was lying on the floor rigid, the paper clutched in her hand; it was impossible to bring her to. He telephoned for Dr. McClaren, who came at once. Floyd told him about the fire in a few words.

"It must have been a great shock to her," said the doctor.

"I don't know," answered Floyd. The doctor looked at him curiously, then went into Julie's room.

He brought her to, insisted on her resting that day in bed, and said to Floyd, "She'll be all right. There's no cause for worry; I've seen her like that before."

Julie believed with all her superstitious, secretive soul, that her hair turning white had been a punishment for giving in to her suppressed passion for Martin; and last night in that very hour of burning joy their house was in flames. "What did it mean? What was that unseen revengeful Power preparing for her?—perhaps another blow, a physical deformity?"

With a cry of terrible fear, she sprang out of bed, locked the door, stood before the long mirror examining herself closely, not like a beautiful woman exulting over her reflected beauty, but with the fear of a guilty soul seeking the brand of further punishment. "What now? What now?" Her body was spotless, like white marble with a delicate tracery of blue veins. She gave a long sigh of relief.

The reporters besieged the house. Floyd had the agony of seeing himself, his wife, his child in every newspaper. The weeklies had colored prints of the beautiful Mrs. Garrison. "She might have stepped out of a picture," "a living Greuze," "the grace of a French Dame de Salon," "the Art of Conversation lives again"—then the Russian players arrived.

Julie did not get over the shock. Her nerves, always abnormal, snapped; she sank into a state of melancholy.

Floyd went up to her room one morning to tell her he wouldn't be home to dinner; she was still in bed, crouching among the pillows.

"Are you waiting for Hippolyte?" There was a touch of irony in his voice.

"I've sent him away. I don't want him any more." Then she broke into sobs.

Floyd was glad to get that "shame" out of the house. Julie was beginning to mope again; she needed fresh air; he would look for a camp in the Adirondacks for the summer.

Julie brooded about her promise to Martin; the revulsion had set in as usual; she was again the mother, the conventional wife. She was afraid of his anger; she must keep away from him. All sorts of horrors took form in her diseased mind.

The clock struck twelve. The boy had gone to the Park with the nurse, a French girl, who spoke little English; they were late. She saw the child run over by a car, lying mangled under the wheels; she was in a paroxysm of fear, a distracted, neurasthenic woman.

"Mamma, see what I've got."

She caught the boy in her arms, passionately kissing his eyes, his mouth, his hair, a handsome fellow, big for his age, his eyes gleaming with excitement.

"Mamma, Mamma!"

He took from Mademoiselle a beautiful, perfectly equipped motor boat.

Mademoiselle explained: "A big dark Monsieur 'belhomme' gave it to Joseph." He said he was his Uncle Martin. He taught him to float and sink it. She couldn't get the child away, that's why they were so late. The boy took the boat to pieces and put it together again, with great dexterity. He was uncommonly intelligent.

"See, Mamma, this is the cabin."

He pressed a spring which opened a little door in the bottom of the boat; within lay a neatly folded paper; the handwriting was Martin's. Mademoiselle took the boy away, looking back furtively with her French comprehension at Madame. A few lines, begging, commanding her to come with the boy the following day.

She knew she would go; she couldn't stay away. He would hold Joseph in his arms; she would take his kisses from the boy's lips; her eyes gleamed. She would go; it would end as it must. She was lost! Hopelessly lost! She went to the Park every day for a week, leaving the maid at home; the boy was always there sailing his boat.

One day Martin took him up suddenly, pressed him in his arms, kissed him again and again. Julie looked on, the blood leaping into her face. They were *her* kisses. Then the boy put his arms around Martin, whispering, "I love you, Uncle Martin," and fell asleep. Martin carried him to the car, motioned Julie to get in first, laid the child beside her, covered him up with the rug, then spoke in low tones of suppressed pain.

"You committed a crime against me, Julie. That boy should have been mine!"

All night and the next day, Julie had one of those terrible headaches; Floyd couldn't bear her moans of pain....

Dr. McClaren took off his coat and goloshes, stopping on the spiral staircase to admire the beautiful colored glass windows. He found Julie crouching in a chair, her hands icy, her eyes roving restlessly.

"My dear Madame, I'm sorry to see you in this nervous state. What is it, tell me? I can't help you unless I know! Is it your husband?"

"No, he is too good."

"The boy, then?"

"No."

"What is troubling you? Tell me."

"Day and night I have a terrible fear that something dreadful is going to happen; I've had it often, but controlled it with a strong effort. Since the night of the fire it has come back with terrible force. I suffer tortures."

"When you go out, do you feel as if someone were following you to do you harm?"

"Yes, yes," she had her eyes fixed on the boat. It seemed to have a terrible fascination for her.

The doctor took the boat from the table, turning it over in his hands. He was thoughtful—puzzled.

"How perfectly they make these toys."

"Yes, it floats and sinks like a real motor boat." The suggestion gave the doctor an idea.

"Do you like the water?"

"Oh, yes."

"Wouldn't you like to take a long sea trip, to Europe, for instance?"

"I would like it very much."

"I'll speak to your husband about it."

"No, no, I don't want him."

"You want to go without him?"

"Yes." He leaned forward to catch her words which came in low gasps. "I want to—to slip away without anybody knowing. If you can persuade Floyd to let me go alone!—you'll find him at his club."

The doctor dropped off at the club that day and spoke to Floyd. He was sitting in the window gazing idly at the green square opposite; what Floyd saw there were flames mounting higher and higher; wherever he went they followed him, scorching him; the world was one great funeral pyre; the flames were drawing him in.

"Your wife is slipping back into the old condition of melancholia; we must prevent that."

"Doctor, I do all I can."

When he suggested a trip to Europe, Floyd gave a quick cry.

"No! no! I couldn't!"

"I want her to go alone." The same look of relief he had seen on Julie's face. A pity; married so short a time. "I would like Miss Mary to go with her, but she is always so busy."

Floyd was on his feet.

"She'll go if I ask her; I'm sure she will."

13

Miss Mary was at home in her little flat on the East Side of downtown. The cry of a newly born child came through the window. She smiled; her ears distinguished the sex. A girl fretted, wailed in a high-pitched, nagging tone; a boy fought, bellowed. Yes, this was a girl. Mary wondered how many men she would make miserable; that would depend on her face. What children men are! They marry a complexion, teeth, eyes. When they get at the woman, it's too late. Some kick over the traces; most of them remain in harness from a sense of honor. The patience married people have with each other is wonderful, considering they are like dice thrown together by accident.

She thought of the Garrisons, and drew two lines on a piece of paper—one a parallel—that stood for *him*; he thought in straight lines. The other, broken with angles—that was *she*. She wondered if he understood that mysterious side of his wife. She saw his eyes, always trying to look happy, his sensitive mouth trying to say pleasant things. A knock at the door startled her; there he stood surrounded by the bare-footed little devils of the neighborhood. They had piloted him up the dark stairs. A little gold-head slipped her hand in his. He bent down and kissed her dirty face; then he distributed all his small change amongst them and shut them out.

"I've had a time finding you, Miss Mary. I've never been in this neighborhood before."

"You should get acquainted with it; it's more interesting than Park Avenue."

"Poverty is terrible."

"No, it's wonderful; it keeps people human. But here there is no poverty; the people earn their living."

"Such as it is." He looked around the room. There was a cot in an alcove, a few chairs, a table, a shelf of books, and she smiling at him.

"You're not feeling well, Mr. Garrison."

"Oh! I'm well enough, but the springs are giving way."

"We must brace them up."

"Impossible, they are broken."

"Then we'll have to get you new springs."

How young she was, how happy, and the bare room; here was—no ego that wants and wants—always taking, never giving—no expectations, no disappointment; Selflessness—that's what kept her so buoyant.

"Can I help you?"

"Yes, if you will."

Then he told her of Julie's relapse and the prescribed sea voyage.

"Dr. McClaren wants her to go without me; he thinks it will be better for her. You know her so well; what is your opinion?"

"Your wife is organically healthy, but there are pathological conditions—a radical change might do her good."

She avoided his eyes; he was disappointed, but what else could she say?

He bent a little nearer.

"Miss Mary, if you will go with her, my mind would be at rest."

She sat silent a moment.

"I'm sorry, but I cannot; I've pledged myself."

"You are engaged?"

She laughed, clapping her hands like a child.

"To be married, you mean? Oh! no! I shall never marry."

He laughed with her, like a boy.

"Not if you fall terribly in love?"

"Not even then!" Her eyes shone defiantly. "I've made a promise to myself, and I won't be a deserter."

"A promise to yourself?"

"Yes, don't you, sometimes?"

"No."

"You should, or life would become too accidental; we would be terribly tossed about."

"That's what's happening to me. I am looking for some occupation, but I don't want to get into a treadmill. The people toil at business, pleasure—they do the same thing day after day, year after year. Life is a habit, a deadening monotony."

She drew up her knees, clasped her hands over them, bent forward. She was a quaint little thing; he had never known anyone like her. She spoke slowly, with difficulty; the words she had at her command couldn't adequately express her thoughts.

"Life is a gift, not a habit. Every day we do the same things, but they must bring us something new in the doing. I've often thought, in the quiet of the sick room, what a privilege it is that I could sit there and help, when all the millions and billions of spirits are crowding the universe, and can't get into life; I'm so glad *I* am put into a body—so happy, so thankful."

"I have never thought it a privilege to live, never thought of life as a gift."

"We depend too much on people and things to make us happy; we shouldn't! Our happiness depends on no one but ourselves."

He knew what she meant. Julie had colored his life for a time; now it was grey.

"I've never thought of it that way."

She came nearer with a touch of eagerness.

"You will, won't you?"

He answered simply:

"Yes, I will—"

Then she went to the table and took up one of a pile of opened letters.

"I have pledged myself to something which will take all my time, all my strength, and that isn't very much."

"No," said Floyd.

"Nursing is gradually becoming a money-making trade. During the War, women seeking adventure with little knowledge were extravagantly paid. Now money is no longer easy, but prices remain high. Only people of means can afford a trained nurse; there is a great need. You don't know how sick people are neglected for want of care. I am trying to bring together earnest women of all classes; there are so many who want to do something, and don't know how. I have appeals from all over the country—piteous cries from women whose lives are empty; their school will be the bedside of the poor. You don't know how quickly they learn, when their heart is in it. They pledge themselves to go wherever they are called, without regard to payment, like the nuns in the early days of Christianity. We are getting together a fund to pay their living. When they are not working they will study, we will have our own home, our own hospital. It has only been whispered, but you have no idea how easy it is to get money." She showed him a letter signed by a well-known millionaire, who guaranteed a large sum. "There are many rich women eager to join us, who are seeking for something better, something nobler in their lives—you don't know—you don't know!"

No, he didn't know!

"I feel very small, annoying you with my personal affairs when you are doing such great things." He made his way to the door. Life was hopeless again.

"Wait."

She was agitated, she couldn't let him go like that; because—she loved him. She knew it now. A wave of gladness rushed through her. She had loved everybody all her life, but this love was like a wonderful magic touch—transporting her into some distant fairy world. She stood by the window; he saw the light on her face.

"I think I can manage it. I want to go to London to the headquarters of the Salvation Army, to Zurich, to confer with the Red Cross Sisters; if your wife will go with me, it will not be neglecting my duty."

He grasped her hand. "Thanks, thanks. I'll never forget this, never."

He saw the blood surging up to her temples, receding, leaving her white. Her eyes were longing, pleading; they sought his. She was beautiful; his heart gave a great bound. He stood looking, looking, stammered something, then turned and went out.

The next few days he was kept busy about the cabins, rugs, passports, exchange. There was a feeling of warmth. He saw Mary standing there with that look in her face; he saw the woman for the first time. How wonderful she was! What a wife she would make! He hoped she wouldn't marry. No man was good enough. He found himself thinking too much about her; then he went and bought something costly for Julie. He refused to stay alone in the house with that French woman. He coaxed Bridget back to take care of the boy while his wife was away. He wondered why Julie didn't write to her friends.

"I don't want anyone to know I am going."

"Not even Maud Dillon?"

"They've moved away somewhere."

He hadn't seen Tom about town as usual. How people disappear when their money is gone and nobody misses them.

The car was waiting at the door. Julie, with a throb of pride, took the boy once more in her arms. The child was beautiful in his velvet suit and lace collar.

"You won't forget me, Joseph?"

"No, Mother."

She placed her photograph on the table beside his little bed.

"You will say good night to me? I will hear it. I will say good night to you; you will hear it."

"Yes, Mother." She put the worn Hebrew prayer book in his hands.

"You will read the prayer I taught you, every morning, every evening?"

"Yes, Mother." The boy's eyes fixed on her face grew deeper; there was a psychic connection between them. She went back to her own childhood. She saw an old man, with that book in his hand, his face lit with religious fervor.

"Julie, you will say the prayer I taught you, every morning, every evening?"

"Yes, Grandfather." She had kept her promise.

The steamer sailed. Mary remained on deck to get a last glimpse of the solitary man standing on the wharf. Julie gave Floyd's flowers to the steward to put on the dining table; there was a bouquet of exquisite red roses in her cabin. When they landed she wore one in her corsage.

14

The earth was thirsty; it poured down for three days, a slow soaking rain. Martin thought it would never stop. He walked along the lake in the Park regardless of his dripping hat. He was aching to see the boy again, to hear him say in his mother's soft voice, "I love you, Uncle Martin." What a mess he had made of his life; now he must steal what rightly belonged to him. He exulted in his power over Julie. Her illness was a fatality; it was her mother's dead hand that had struck her daughter down to save her from him. A shiver ran through him; why was he so superstitious? He didn't believe in anything—but sometimes a peculiar feeling took hold of him; there was another life far back, a mystery—something intangible. He walked hours in the rain—fighting invisible forces, cursing the conditions of his life; it all resolved itself back to the same determination. She had promised to go with him; she must keep her word.

Towards evening he rang the side-door bell at Hippolyte's, hoping to get some news of her. The dark-skinned valet whisked off his coat, dried his dripping hair and neck, and preceded him into the Turkish room behind the shop. It was Hippolyte's hour of rest before the night's activity; he was lying on a divan, a picturesque figure, in a loose red silk robe. He waved Martin a welcome with his small white hand, the diamond, set in platinum on his finger, flashing rose color in the soft electric glow of the pervading red.

"*Sapristi*, Monsieur Steele. I was thinking of you."

Martin dropped down in a deep chair, stretched out his legs. The aroma of coffee and a whiff of perfumed opium lent a sense of warmth to his chilled body.

"Of me? Are you in trouble again?"

His pipe-dream-visions changed into the cold reality of a check book; he had often helped the man out of his financial difficulties, he earned enormous sums, but the overhead expenses were fabulous.

"The money is nothing; it comes in and goes out like the tide. I am at the end, the compass changes. We must in Life watch for the Warning. We must train our ear to detect the direction of the wind."

"You are superstitious?"

"We all are, if we knew its true meaning. Superstition is an intense sense of the Invisible."

Martin drank the strong Turkish coffee, puffing at his chibouk. The man was a "hairdresser," but that didn't matter; Martin had no sense of class.

"My time in this business will soon be over. I was the only one for years when it was an 'elite' profession. Now it is vulgarized like everything else. There is a clever Russian woman who is taking all my customers; do you know why? The husbands are jealous."

Martin laughed—he understood that; he would never allow this fascinating, purring Greek to maul *his* wife about.

"*Mon ami*, I know what you are thinking; you are wrong. They talk a great deal about the immorality of the American woman. It is not so—and it is a shame that it is not so. The French woman is honest; she have her husband, her lover; he has his wife, his mistress. Marriage is a success in France; they do not go about divorcing themselves. Here marriage is a failure, because every woman, young, middle age, old, talk of love!—it is only talk!—*mon ami*, talk! talk!—but she *do* nothing! nothing! Why! because she is afraid; the fear is in her blood from the old times in America, the fear of the 'Scarlet Letter.' Oh! she can love, *Mon Dieu*! and if by accident there is just a little false step, she make a scene, her relatives make a scene, the press make a scene, everybody make a scene. Oh! your Hawthorne did not know what harm he was doing to the future women of his country. The French authors knew better. La nouvelle Heloise—Camille, the heroines of de Maupassant, have set the women of France a glorious example."

Martin smiled. The fellow was clever, insolent.

"Do you know how it will end?"

"No, my imagination doesn't take me any farther."

"Bah!—it is easy, she will go back to the pale face and the straight hair. You will see the little Puritan again. They have already forbid us the wine, the splendid opium, the tobacco, silk stockings, cosmetics, love—the whole nation will go to bed at nine o'clock—and their money will choke them."

Martin laughed, but the man was very serious; he put his hand on Martin's shoulder.

"*Mon ami*, you have been good to me. You know the Figaro has the soul of an artist; I am going to be good to you. I am going to tell you something you do not know; Mrs. Garrison will sail Saturday for England, without her husband."

15

The Garrison "shanties," near the river, were kept in as good condition as possible, but time and rats gnawed at their foundations. On one of these the passer could read, with some difficulty, the faded letters of an old sign, "Martin Steele and Son, Established 1830."

Since Mr. Steele's death, the business had been carried on by a Mr. Waldbridge, who knew and followed the old conservative methods of the defunct Steeles. Young Mr. Steele was expected to take his father's place as head of the firm, but he stayed away, took what money he wanted, a ridiculously small amount for a man of his means, leaving the surplus in the business. Waldbridge had written several times asking him to come down and look over the books. Finally, he appeared. He was a mystery to Mr. Waldbridge; all the young business men of the day were eager speculators. He had expected new ideas, a business revolution; but no such things happened. He would sit about, watch closely the proceedings, but made no suggestions. His visits grew less and less frequent.

"What does he do with himself?" thought Mr. Waldbridge. "He doesn't gamble. He's never seen at the races or baseball games. His name has never been connected with women. What kind of a man is he?"

Martin sat opposite him in the private office, flung his soft hat on the floor, crossed his long legs; his hair was disarranged, his face a yellow pallor; his clothes hung loosely, he was very thin. His "appearance" struck Mr. Waldbridge as very un-American—he himself being an Erie Road commuter with all the proud consciousness of a one hundred per cent Nationalism.

He spoke cautiously of the hard times and unsatisfactory business conditions. They had advanced money on large stocks of merchandise; there was nothing to do but to hold on. If they forced the sale, it would mean enormous losses.

"Yes, I know," interrupted Martin impatiently. "We couldn't go on gorging money at that rate; we'd have to vomit it up sometime. No stomach could hold it; that's what we're doing now. Some people die suddenly from it; we'll have a lingering end."

Waldbridge laughed uneasily, really a very unpleasant young man.

"I hope we will weather it. I've been discounting—and—"

Martin interrupted again—discounting meant nothing to him—although he was flying some moral "kites" on his own account.

"Do whatever you like; I'm out of it."

Waldbridge rose to his feet.

"What do you mean?"

"You can take my father's name down."

"If you liquidate the business now, it will mean disaster."

"I have no interest in it. I am leaving New York."

Then Waldbridge broke down. It was terrible, a long-established, respected firm—wreckage—pure wreckage; that word seemed to have a fatal significance in Martin's life.

"Can I count on, say, ten thousand a year for ten years?"

Julie was luxuriously inclined, because her heart had been empty. He would take her away from cities; they would live somewhere quietly in the country.

Waldbridge smiled. "You can always have that and more if you want it."

Then Martin did a wonderful thing, so wonderful it left Waldbridge speechless, staring at him. Was the man mad? There was a taint of insanity in the family.

Martin read his thoughts.

"I'm thirty-two years old, and I know what I am doing. I want you to turn this business into a company; every man in it, from the lowest to the highest, must have his share. You, of course, will be the head of the firm. Get a good lawyer and do it legally. You'll have your work, every mother's son of you, to get the old hulk out of the mud; if you do, you're entitled to the spoils."

"And the capital?" gasped Waldbridge.

"I told you what I want, the rest I'll leave in business; you can't go on without it, can you?"

"No."

"Then what's the use of talking about it."

He held out his hand; Waldbridge grasped it, trying to stammer out his gratitude, but Martin was gone. He dashed out of the place, threw himself into a taxi.

"Uptown."

The New York chauffeur is accustomed to indefinite addresses. He looked back at the man with his hat pulled over his eyes, crouching in a corner. "A bloke who had lost his wad." Then he wondered if it was a defaulter or a gunman—some of them looked like perfect gentlemen. He drove uptown, entered the Park. There he stopped. He was hungry; that guy in the corner could sleep all day.

"Where to?"

Martin, pitched forward by the sudden jolt, glared at him.

"The Waldorf."

He sprang up the stairs three at a time, too nervous to wait for the elevator, looked around the room, which was in disorder; his man couldn't keep it tidy. Martin flung everything about.

He would take nothing with him but a dress suit case. He caught sight in the corner of an old box covered with deerskin, tied together with a thick rope; he had taken it from the garret after his grandfather's death, but had never opened it. He untwisted the knots, one after the other. It was a hard job. It hurt his fingers. He took out a pair of mountain boots, goat's leather, with large nails in the soles. Martin looked down at his feet; they would fit him. He pulled out an old woollen shirt, a pair of corduroy trousers, a felt hat with a green feather, a bright colored vest, and red handkerchiefs. There was a small chamois bag with strange coins, Swiss money—Martin examined them curiously; a pack of old letters, a photograph of a young boy and girl, a cow, and a high mountain at the back. That mountain fascinated him; he looked at it long, intensely. The raw boy and girl in Swiss dress were his grandparents. Martin thought of his mother. On the back of the card there was something printed which he made out with difficulty: "Val Sinestra." He had never heard the name. He put everything back in the trunk and roped it; the idea came suddenly: he would take it with him, to Switzerland.

16

After Julie left, Floyd spent his evenings at the club; there were many strange to him. The membership had increased; it was still a mark of class to be seen lounging at the club-window in the afternoon.

He missed Martin. He was different from the others. When he raved against the world, he said things in bad taste, but often the bitter truth. With a sudden impulse, he wrote a few lines, asking him to lunch at the club the following day. He'd be furious when he heard Julie had sailed. He'd say, "You might have given me a chance to send her a few flowers." Floyd smiled; yes, he liked Martin; more than that, he loved him; he was interwoven with the memories of his childhood, his youth. He wished that episode had not happened when Julie was ill, but she was unconscious of it. She had never in all that time mentioned his name. It was all in his own evil mind. He mentally asked pardon of Martin. The next morning at breakfast he had a feeling of agreeable expectancy.

The boy was crying upstairs. Bridget couldn't quiet him.

"What's the matter up there?"

The child fretted for his mother. He had caught a cold, and had been kept in the house for some days. He was standing with his boat in his hands, sobbing piteously. Floyd pacified him by running the water into the bath which was sunken in the center of a tiled room. The boy handed his father the boat.

Floyd turned it over in his hand.

"A costly toy. Mamma is good to you."

"Mamma didn't give it to me."

"Yes she did—Mamma gives you everything."

"She didn't," insisted the boy. "My Uncle Martin bought it for me."

"Your Uncle Martin?"

"Yes. He came every day to the Park, and then he put a note in the cabin, telling Mamma to come, and she came."

"Where is the cabin?"

"You can't find it, nobody but me."

The boy in great glee pressed the spring.

"There's no letter there!"

"Oh! no! I gave it to Mamma; she read it and tore it up."

Floyd pushed the boy away. He was making a spy of his innocent child. Why didn't Julie tell him?

"Did Mamma meet Uncle Martin in the Park every day?"

"No, not every day; she'd stay away sometimes because Uncle Martin scolded her and she'd cry. He loved me and petted me and said he was going to steal me away."

"But you wouldn't leave me, would you, Joseph?"

The boy meditated, and then told the truth.

"Perhaps I would, Papa, if Mamma came along; but I don't think she'd come because Uncle Martin scolded her too much. I was mad at him and said 'Uncle Martin, you'll have to beg Mother's pardon; I always do when I'm bad.' Then Uncle Martin laughed and gave me such a long kiss and said, 'There, take that to Mamma and it will be all right.'"

Floyd sat motionless with the boy in his arms. The little fellow's eyes drooped, he slid down, pillowed his head on the big fur animal; those glassy eyes brought Floyd back to Mrs. Gonzola—why did she always watch Julie? He had never asked any questions about the unexpected call on the telephone. He had been deliriously happy; there was no room in his thoughts for the past.

He bent over the child, noting the beautiful powerful body; neither he nor Julie had great physical strength. The boy would be a giant. Why did Mrs. Gonzola press such a quick marriage? Why did she keep him away so much during their short engagement? Why did she want Julie to get "used" to the idea? As a child Julie liked Martin better; they'd disappear and he'd wander about looking for them, then go home disappointed. In his mad desire to get her, he had really done Martin an injustice; he should have waited. He didn't do the square thing, because—he knew Martin would have won out! He bent lower over the boy—trying to find some clue in that innocent face! The blood rushed to his head—he must have it out with Martin—he couldn't go on with evil suspicions of his wife, his friend. Martin was no liar! He always told the brutal truth, even if it were against himself.

The night brought sanity, consolation. Julie was foolish, but not criminal. Her religion wouldn't let her do anything wrong. She went to Confession the day before her marriage; then he wondered—what did she really believe? She was by creed a Catholic, but she taught her boy his prayers in Hebrew.

He went early to the club and waited for Martin, who was late as usual. He looked at his watch, and idly took up the morning paper.

His eye caught a headline. "The *Aquitania* sailing with a distinguished crowd on board."

What! the ship already back and sailing again? It was the usual summer rush; he knew most of the names. One riveted his gaze. He read it once, twice, three times; the paper dropped from his hand. He saw that name wherever he looked. Martin Steele had sailed on the *Aquitania*.

It was ten days before the next steamer crowded with pleasure-seekers sailed for England. At the last moment Floyd came on board, too late to have his name in the passenger list. The only cabin left was on the lowest deck inside. He went down, locked the door, unpacked his valise. Most of its space was taken up by a silver-mounted leather box—one would say an elegant toilette case. He opened it, took out a brace of shining pistols, examined each one carefully, and put it back in the box. He had no definite plan, but when a man catches a thief in his house he shoots him....

17

Martin arrived in London and put up at the Savoy; he noticed the crowds of fine young fellows and beautifully dressed women.

"Is there anything unusual going on tonight?"

"Yes," said the polite young clerk, "a dinner and dance, in honor of Mrs. Garrison, an American lady."

Julie had been received by the Ambassador in London with great cordiality, on account of his old friendship for Jimmie Garrison. Mary wrote to Mr. Garrison:

You have all reason to be well satisfied with your wife. We have done the right thing. She is enjoying herself. She looks like a young girl; the element which disturbed her has disappeared. I find her so much more normal.

The letter never reached Floyd.

Martin stood in the doorway, his eyes fixed on Julie, who was surrounded by eager applicants, waiting their turn to dance with the "silver-haired beauty." He took in the soft white neck, the dimpled arms, the small classic head, and that something in the curve of her mouth and yielding smile—a triumphant sensuality. She swept past him. He could have touched her; he stood motionless.

Mary was up early the next morning. She stood looking at Julie, in a deep sleep, her hair falling loose, enveloping her in a veil of unreality; then she shut the door softly and went into the salon. Waiting for her simple breakfast, she watched the passing busses and pedestrians in the street below. All large cities are the same, but different, like people; each individuality giving another form to the Image or material symbol. London has a distinct personality; nobility of character is unmistakably stamped upon it.

The door opened; she turned and saw Martin. There was a momentary fear; then she was her quiet self again. Martin apologized for startling her. They measured each other; he saw an enemy.

"Why are you so antagonistic to me?"

"I'm never antagonistic without reason?"

"What reason have I given you?"

- 89 -

She looked keenly at him. He was well groomed—a clean-shaven, intense face, fascinating for some women; he repelled Mary. He has courage to show his mouth, she thought.

"I have been sent here by Mrs. Garrison's doctor; she has had a serious illness, you know that."

"Yes."

"She may at any time fall back into the same condition. I don't want her to know you are here."

"Why?"

There was a gleam of humor in his eyes; it angered her. Why should she play policy with him?

"Because your presence may excite her. You are Mr. Garrison's friend. I hope you will take my advice and not try to see her until she has finished her cure."

"What cure?"

"She has been sent to a place in Switzerland called Val Sinestra, to drink arsenic water; you see I am keeping nothing from you."

"Very kind, I could easily find out. Val Sinestra?" The name was familiar.

She stood with her hand on the door-knob waiting for him to go.

"Val Sinestra. I will write her."

"I have orders to withhold any communications which may excite her."

"Orders from her husband?"

"No, from her doctor."

Her eyes shot fire at him....

He went back to his room, took out of his bag the bundle of old letters. Yes, that was the name, "Val Sinestra"; it was Destiny.

There were two sides to Martin: a fiercely brutal realism, and a mysticism, instinctively concealed. As a boy, he would lie night after night, his eyes wide open; visions came and faded. It was always the same struggle with an unseen horror. He would awaken from a restless sleep, his face damp with tears. Those days he was very silent; his stepmother called them his sullen fits. As he grew older the visions vanished, but he had hours of deep abstraction, when reality slipped away from him.

He sat in his room, the banal colored post-card of the two young peasants in his hand. There was a sudden consciousness of Liberation; the other self flew out and away through walls, over seas, over mountain peaks, soaring, soaring. He sat there for hours motionless.

That evening the hotel clerk handed Miss Mary a note. It contained one line scrawled on half a sheet of paper.

"Am leaving for Paris."

She was very glad, she wondered how far it had gone between those two. The responsibility was heavy.

18

At thirty-two Martin put his foot for the first time upon the soil of his ancestors. He roamed through Zurich; mounted its narrow cobble-stoned alley-ways, stood before an overhanging house reading the inscription. "This house is three hundred years old." The lives of Zwingli, Pestalozzi became familiar. He read ravenously the history of the town. He stood on the border of its blue lake, encircled with snow mountains, "A Turquoise on a white bosom." Something stirred in him, an inward convulsion, like the sudden eruption of an extinct crater; he broke into choking tearless sobs. Martin, unknown to himself, had the Swiss temperament—a people without the gift of self-expression, a deeply religious peasant race, silent before the mystic beauty of their mountains. Patriotism, that misunderstood word, with its medieval clashing of swords, its uniforms, its medals, has no relation to the Swiss adoration of the soil. He worships his valleys, his lakes, his waterfalls; they are living to him; he has a rage for the mountains; he leaves his country to seek wealth, but he rarely stays in the stranger's land; nostalgia drives him home; he must get back to the heights or die. Martin understood later why his grandfather went mad, why his father was wordless, why his mother died young.

He tried his Swiss on the *portier* of the Bauer au lac Hotel, a man of all-round information, a veritable encyclopædia of Switzerland, who could answer in the many languages of the cosmopolitan crowd, on its way to and from the mountains. Martin spoke a few words to him in his grandfather's "lingo," then said, "What am I speaking, anyhow?"

"Your dialect is Romontsch or Romance. Your people came from the Grisons."

Then he explained how in the Middle Ages the Barons and Bishops had oppressed the people, and how they formed Leagues and fought for their freedom. The Grisons took their name from the "Gray League," a heroic band of peasants.

Martin left Zurich by the early train the next morning; he sat the entire day gazing out of the window unconscious of the other passengers. A great moving picture shot before him—green valleys, velvet hills, beautiful grazing animals, brooks changing into waterfalls, cataracts dashing down dark ravines, mountains growing higher, higher. At Tarasp he stayed over night to connect with the stage-coach at daybreak, and spent the evening sitting outside with the guides, who told him of the Val Sinestra, where the bandits used to live in caves, deep down in the ravines, and smuggled wine over the border. Then they spoke in lowered tones of the danger of mountain climbing—of death—of miracles they had seen above in the mist, with their own eyes.

With the rising of the sun, seated beside the coach driver, Martin pierced the mountain passes; they stopped at a quaint hamlet.

"We turn here," said the old man. Then he wished "Godspeed," cracked his whip, and went on. The coach pitched from side to side, on a perilously narrow road, but the horses were sure-footed, and the driver, past seventy, had gone the same way for fifty years.

Martin drew deep breaths of the fragrant air; he looked about him. The houses were a mixture of old Swiss and Italian architecture—the protruding windows and little balconies were covered with bright flowers; in the distance he caught sight of a picturesque church and cemetery. He entered an inn with a swinging sign; a rooster flapping its wings. The spotless floors sprinkled with sand, the small counter with shelves of bottles, the peasant girl in the costume of the Canton—it was all so familiar. She brought him a glass of wine and a pretzel, smiling at his jargon. He remarked on the absence of men.

"They are 'up there' with the cows for the summer." She pointed to the green hills, gradually becoming steeper. "In those little huts on the top they make the cheese which they send all over the world. In the winter the sun doesn't come up very high; it is like a blue twilight here. The storms howl, the snow falls for weeks. When the peasant closes his eyes, the avalanche haunts him; if he awakens in the morning he is grateful to God." The girl went on chattering in her soft "Romance." "The doctor goes down to Croire in the winter, but our pastor stays with us. We have service here when the snow is too deep to walk to the chapel." Then she put down the glass she was polishing, and went joyously to the door to meet a tall man, a gigantic peasant, with masses of thick gray hair falling to his shoulder. He was long past seventy, but showed no signs of age. His voice rang out stentorian, clear. He was warm, wiping the perspiration from his face with a large red handkerchief. He looked at Martin with keen penetrating eyes. Then said, "Good morning."

"Oh, you speak English."

"Yes, we have many English visitors. Our children are taught it in the schools." He looked again, seemingly puzzled.

"What is your name?"

"Martin Steele. My people come from over here."

"Steele." He shook his head. "I know none of that name."

Martin took from his pocket the bundle of old letters. One glance at them and the pastor's arms were around him.

"I wrote those letters to your grandfather. I am his brother. You are not an American, you are a Swiss. Your name is not Steele, it is Staehli—Martin Staehli. The eldest of our family, for generations back, was always Martin."

Martin felt a throb of joy; the blood of this fine old man with the head of a Roman ran in his veins. He had known only Aunt Priscilla, whom he wanted to burn.

"Come, I am going to take you home with me."

Martin looked back at the Swiss "Madel." In her red skirt and velvet bodice— an image of national womanhood.

They walked together down the hill, through the fields, past the little chapel and cemetery where they stopped. On the headstones he read again and again the name, "Martin Staehli." He would bring his grandfather, his parents and lay them where they belonged, and he would lie there beside them.

The pastor looked up at the great mountain, already casting a shadow over the valley; even in summer the day was short. The night came early and lingered.

"We are not all here. My son was the best guide in the Canton. He was lost in a snow-drift up there."

At the châlet with its black beams, centuries old, still strong, unyielding, he put his hand over Martin's head and blessed his entrance into the home of his fathers.

Martin stood in the long hall, vaguely conscious of atmosphere. A cuckoo sprang out of an old clock, chanting the hour; a spinning wheel with threaded flax; new linen piled up; a living thing, that wheel, it clothed the people. Carved chests, plaques of fruit, birds cut out by the natives, when the country was Italian—everything in the room bearing witness,—a living story-teller of the lives and times of the vanished family. For the first time he *felt* the antique. He was swayed by a kind of psychic storm, like a rush of wind through the pass of a mountain.

The pastor at the door called, "Angela, Angela."

A clear voice answered; she came down the path—a girl of sixteen, with bits of hay in her flaxen hair, a child-like look of wonder in her blue eyes, and something more—of mystery. Martin thought of Joan of Arc in the orchard.

On seeing Martin, she gave a quick impulsive cry. The pastor put his arm around her.

"What frightens you, Angela? It is my brother, Martin's son from America."

Angela extended her hand, but her warm radiance had vanished. "Come out in the sun, it is cold here."

She brought mugs of thick yellow milk, brown bread, delicious chipped beef, then went again into the field and sat sorting out leaves from a basket. The pastor followed Martin's gaze which lingered on the girl; she appealed to his artistic sense.

"Angela is a wonder child; she is not of our family. I found her one moonlit winter night in a snow-drift—a white angel. Since she came the village has prospered; the people are happy."

Martin smiled: probably the child of some unfortunate village girl. The pastor read his thoughts. "She belongs to no one; she is a miracle-child. You don't believe in miracles?"

"No."

"Then why are you here?"

A simple question, difficult to answer. He couldn't express the longing, which from childhood had made him restless, unhappy—a longing for some other space, some other element. He couldn't explain his agitation, his unbearable joy, when he saw those scenes of which his grandfather had babbled in incoherent broken bits. He answered conventionally.

"I wanted to see the place where my grandfather was born."

The pastor grew very serious. "It was not a case of idle curiosity you were drawn here; Angela knew you were coming. I used to tell her stories of your grandfather, Martin Staehli. He was queer; had a streak in him of evil. He got into a brawl with a guide and killed him; he had to leave the country."

"I never knew that," said Martin.

"That's why he changed his name. I wrote to him often, but he seldom answered. Poor Martin, he got very rich."

Martin laughed bitterly. That almost uncontrollable instinct to destroy was his inheritance.

"Angela said the third generation would return home. She has the gift of prophecy and of healing. She cures the people of their ills. The cattle run to her for her herbs; there is a magic in them. She brews them with Prayer, with Love."

Martin shook off a peculiar feeling; it was all superstitious nonsense, an insult to a man's intelligence. He rose to go.

"You will stay here with us?"

"I'm sorry, but I must meet some friends. Where is the Val Sinestra Hotel?"

"A little distance from here, on the other side of the hill beyond the hay-field."

Martin looked up at the straight stony walls of the big mountain.

"I'm going to climb that mountain," he said.

The pastor smiled. "Perhaps, when you have had long practice; a man must train himself to climb."

The pastor watched him as he went with quick uneven steps, stumbling here and there; he had no equilibrium. He'd never climb that mountain.

Angela was also watching Martin. The pastor put his hand on her shoulder; she started.

"He terrifies me; I am afraid of him." She threw herself sobbing into the old man's arms.

19

The pale women were coming up from the Springs, where they drank the arsenic water with a prayer for red corpuscles, strength, beauty. The Spring of Youth was in a cleft in the mountain—a dark mysterious fountain of gushing water unlit by the sun.

Martin paced his room in the hotel. She was there, arrived two weeks before; the cure was nearly over. The madness came back now; he had been free of it for a few hours. It was like the relapse of a fever, violent—vicious—raging. He had waited too long for her with stupid patience, and more stupid scruples. He heard Julie's voice downstairs; he went to the window. She was standing on the terrace talking to Miss Mary, who was leaving. She kissed Julie, jumped into the hotel omnibus, and drove off. Julie stood a moment waving her hand, then turned and entered the house. He heard her voice outside in the corridor speaking to the maid. The next door opened; her room adjoined his.

The Sun-God sinking slowly behind the mountain scattered an orgy of color. Julie stepped out on her balcony. There was a low railing between them. He jumped over.

"Julie!"

She started with sudden fear, fled into the room. He followed, tried to say something, stood speechless looking at her. She was wonderful. The force of the rich blood surging under the white skin swept him like a cyclone. There was a new intensity of life in her, quick flashes of passion in her eyes. She gave a low cry, threw her arms out trembling with uncontrollable joy.

"You! You!" She kissed him again and again. How she kissed him! then drew him outside.

"Come! come! The sun is setting; it was too wonderful, I couldn't bear it alone." His eyes held hers.

"I saw Miss Mary driving away."

"Yes, she has gone to Tarasp to visit an old patient; she will be away until tomorrow afternoon."

A shadow fell; it was twilight.

"You must go now."

He tried to hold her; she slipped out of his arms, shutting the long windows after her. He went back to his room. Those fleeting moments made him eager, desperate. The night was coming on; they were alone together at the end of the world.

Miss Mary sitting in the train was troubled. She opened a telegram and read it again, "Meet me at Tarasp. Say nothing to my wife. Floyd Garrison."

20

The little parlor of the hotel was filled with guests, assembled there, as was the custom, waiting for the dining-room doors to be opened. Martin, standing in the hall, a living symbol of electric force, created a sensation. He drew nearer and took in the crowd of pale women, young, nervous, with mysterious ills they could not, or would not, explain to their doctor, who, for the lack of a suitable name, called the sickness "anæmia." He looked them over with an experienced man's compelling eyes. Some were very good-looking, would have been beautiful under favorable conditions, but they were pale, with white lips and drawn features, like plants in a dark cellar pining for the sun. He became amusedly conscious of being the only man; he finally espied in the garden a rheumatic old fellow, like the decayed trunk of a tree.

He felt a battery of admiring glances leveled at him. He smiled, went to the foot of the staircase, waited for Julie.

They went in to dinner together. The table in a deep window at the far end of the room was decorated tonight with an abundance of flowers. Martin played with his food; he was too excited to eat, but he was in wonderful spirits. Julie had never seen him like that; she had a feeling of triumphant elation. He was handsome; the other women were envying her.

He laughingly remarked about the Eden with one Adam and many temptresses.

"They are all so white, as if frozen in ice; the Sun-God should come and melt them." He squeezed her hand under the table. "I am sorry for the 'good' women. They sacrifice themselves for an illusion—chastity."

She answered quickly. "The woman doesn't think so. It is her religion. It may mean nothing to you, but for her it is a spiritual compensation."

"Oh, that's Catholic," laughed Martin. She shivered, drew her cape around her.

Then he said, "Look how beautiful! The twilight is wonderful up here, light mixing with darkness like two souls. How the valley stretches out. Do you hear the rushing of waters? They are saying, 'Give me your body, I will heal you.' Look! The mountain has a halo of red; it catches at my throat and chokes me...."

He was poetic, inspired. He raised his glass. "The wine goes through my veins like warm blood. If I were a doctor, I'd prescribe it for the ladies."

"Oh, oh," laughed Julie, "forbidden fruit!"

"And you?" There was a laughing question in his eyes.

"I'm cured." She drained the glass.

After dinner they walked up and down the terrace in front of the hotel, like old friends who had not met for some time and had much to say to each other. Gradually, the buzzing inside subsided, the pale creatures evaporated, lights were put out; one glimmered in each corridor.

He drew Julie into a small summer house covered with vines, at the end of the garden. The head waitress brought in wine. He thanked her—the Swiss know the hotel business. He slipped his arm under Julie's cape. She resisted, but he held her close. She could hear his heart beating violently. Then it seemed as if it stood quite still, but it commenced soon to hammer again against hers.

"I must go in," she whispered. "They close the house early." She put her arms around his neck, raised her face to his.

"How dark it is."

"Yes. It's always so before the moon comes up." Then she slipped away. He caught her back.

"Will you give me a signal?" It was a moment of suspense.

"Yes."

He looked up at her room; there was a candle burning in the window.

"When you put out that light, I'll come."

He reluctantly let her go. She went up the stairs; he saw her at her window. There was a white spirit also watching—the moon, that "Orbèd Maiden," chaste as the sleeping women within. Only those two were living; with them it was Flood-Tide.

The light in Julie's window went out. It was dark now, the moon ashamed had turned away her face. He started to go; his feet were lead; his body weighed them down. What ailed him? He shook himself like an angry beast.

"Martin, don't go."

The voice was low, but very clear; did it come from without or within? He didn't know.

"Martin, don't commit this crime; don't rob your friend. If you love the woman, do not destroy her; it is one throb more, one desire fulfilled—and then—the Price...."

At daybreak, the gardener, crawling about, found the stranger in the summer house, his head on the table, buried in his arms. He looked at the empty bottles. The wine of the Canton was strong; he shook the sleeping man, once, twice. Martin started up; where was he?...

The hotel was empty. The guests were at the Springs. A bath of mineral effervescent water refreshed him, but that strange feeling came again like a dream which returns in fitful flashes, fragments of color impossible to blend. He paced the room; his eyes fell upon the deerskin trunk he had brought with him. He opened it, took out the corduroy trousers, boots, shirt— examined them critically. His valet had pronounced them "only fit for the ash can," but that didn't influence Martin. He had them cleaned, folded, and put back into the box. He drew on the soft leather boots; they fitted him. The woollen shirt was light and warm. Looking at himself in the glass, he saw a man of the mountains—real, living. If a man buys a costume like that, it is only a masquerade; this was his inheritance.

The omnibus came back from the Springs; he went down and helped Julie out, seeking in her face the reproach he deserved. She smiled at him; how sweet of her! The fact was, when Julie reached her room the usual revulsion of feeling set in. She undressed quickly, dropping her clothing in a heap on the floor, blew out the candle. There was a dark form below—waiting—she stood breathless, her hand on the knob of the door. Then—she turned the key, crept to the window, pushed the bolt. She was securely locked in—she slipped into bed.

This morning she looked very girlish in a sport suit; the short skirt grazing the tops of very high tan leather boots. A soft hat, pulled down over one eye, gave her rosy face a touch of diablerie. She was all animation, joking about his Alpine costume, casting roguish glances at him; but he felt the undercurrent of emotion. He adored her.

"We are going out for a day in the woods."

"You don't ask, will I go."

"No—but you will, won't you?"

There was pathos in his voice, longing; she couldn't resist him.

"Yes, but I must rest after the bath and dress lightly. The morning here is cold; at noon it gets very warm."

He bent down and whispered, "Wear white like a bride."

During the interval of waiting, Martin studied a map of the Canton, tracing lines from one Dorf to another, short walking tours through the woods; there were plenty of little inns where they could rest. He paced the terrace impatiently.

She came, all in white. A filmy scarf wound around her head, "à la turque," accentuated the Oriental in her. She laughingly drew the long floating streamers across her face; her eyes shot fire through their soft transparency.

A little wagon drove up; the peasant boy cracked his whip and they started off. The road was smooth, sunlit. They stopped at the Springs, where Julie made him drink the unsavory water "to clear his complexion." They were in high spirits, laughing at simple things, like two children. When they reached the chasm, the road became steep, narrow, with dark overhanging trees. Martin drew Julie close to him; a mysterious something hovered about them, intangible in its beauty, penetrating, wonderful.

The driveway ended there. The descent into the ravine must be finished on foot. The lad took a basket from the wagon and set it on the ground; then he cracked his whip and drove off.

21

At the Savoy, Floyd heard many flattering things about his beautiful wife. He was silent, kept turning over the pages of the hotel register, finally found the name he was looking for—"Martin Steele, New York." Then he wired Miss Mary and left at once for Switzerland, made quick connections, arriving at Tarasp toward evening. The stage-coach from Val Sinestra was expected. He paced up and down before the hotel, his thoughts stinging like a swarm of bees.

He had married well, he was a happy man—in the world's vocabulary.

Happy? A man who marries Beauty lives on a powder mine. The something which compels adoration makes a woman unfit for matrimony. A man can't always be on his knees; that's very well at night—but he becomes a ridiculous figure in the daylight.

The coach shambled up the road. Mary was the only passenger; she nodded and smiled at him. He helped her out.

"Were you surprised to get my telegram?"

"Yes."

"You understood?"

Mary waited. She wasn't sure how much he knew.

He spoke again excitedly.

"Why did Dr. McClaren send my wife to Europe without me?"

"Mrs. Garrison wanted it; there was no peace for her with that man so near."

He was watching her keenly. Did he think she was in collusion with his wife against him? Her face burned; she looked straight at him.

"Mr. Garrison, it was an experiment and very successful. She is cured."

He was ashamed. She and the doctor knew his dishonor, and then—the world. His voice was hot—angry.

"He followed her to London; they were together at the Savoy."

"No!"

"He was there."

Then she told him of her encounter with Martin, and how he went away without seeing Julie.

He had done them a terrible injustice? He was piteously grateful, held her hands, made a foolish attempt to kiss them. She grew very pale, and said, "Oh! Mr. Garrison!" He dropped them, very much embarrassed, looked at his watch. It was already ten o'clock; the evening had passed quickly, in spite of his misery.

"You are tired. I have been inconsiderate."

"Oh no, but if you don't mind, I'll go to my room now."

He stood at the foot of the stairs looking after her; she smiled back at him. She was glad she had been able to bring him a hopeful message.

They started off the next morning, in a comfortable open carriage. Mary told him funny stories about the "blood-poor" women and their arsenic intoxication, showed him pretty twists in the splendid road built by the Romans. They stopped at a little inn for a bite of cheese and a glass of beer. He planned a trip to Lugano and over the lake to Italy; he was in good spirits; the sense of relief acted like a strong stimulant.

Mary was very loyal to Julie.

"Mr. Garrison, I can assure you everything is all right. I have written to Rome at Mrs. Garrison's request. After her cure she has plans to go with you to visit Father Cabello."

Floyd was very penitent.

"I am glad to know that. Father Cabello has a strong influence over my wife. She has been too worldly; I hope he will bring her back to religion."

On arriving at the hotel, Mary went at once to Julie's room; it was in great disorder—everything scattered about, as if she had dressed very hurriedly. Floyd downstairs was questioning the woman manager.

"Madame had gone with Monsieur Steele; they had taken luncheon with them. Did Madame expect Monsieur Garrison?"

"No. I wanted to surprise her. Do you know where they went?"

"Yes. The boy who drove them is here."

"I would like to find them, if possible."

The woman went to order the wagon.

Mary was pale, agitated.

"Mr. Garrison, when I left your wife, Mr. Steele was not here."

He didn't answer; he frightened her.

"What are you going to do?"

"Find her and bring her back."

"A storm is brewing," said the woman. "They come up quickly and are terrible while they last."

The wagon drove up; he jumped in. Mary stood watching him till he was out of sight. The clouds gathered; the wind slunk into its den.

Floyd pushed back his hat, wiped the perspiration from his forehead; it was stifling.

22

The lovers stood together on a grassy plateau, the sun poured bright beams of light; below was a dense mist.

"How wonderful," said Martin. "Nature has kept a sunny spot for us; we'll stay here awhile." He drew his "lodin" cape around him, stretched himself out on the grass, looking up at the golden clouds surrounding the sun, looking below at the rapidly rising veil of gray; it was glorious.

Julie took bread, fowl, wine out of the basket; they ate with their fingers and drank the wine out of the bottle. The sun glimmered red through the dark clouds. They were silent; then he spoke, quietly at first, becoming gradually very much excited.

"Why did you throw me over so heartlessly, after you promised me to prepare your mother? I knew it was useless; I had made all my arrangements—I had a cabin engaged on a French steamer—"

Julie tried to justify herself, then began to cry hysterically; she had never broken faith with him. He couldn't imagine what she'd been through all her life. The pressure of those two terrible religions: her grandfather dragging her one way, her mother threatening her with eternal punishment.

He tried to soothe her.

"Don't cry, Julie, I'll make it up to you. You will be happy for the first time in your life."

"But Floyd—he's been so good—you always came between us, pushing him away."

She slipped out of his arms. It was Floyd now coming between them, it wasn't so easy to push *him* away. They had been friends so long. Floyd was the innocent victim. Martin's eyes roved restlessly—and that gray mist—rising!—rising!

She waited for him to speak; then she went to him like a child, piteous, pathetic.

"Martin, don't be angry with me—I love you—but the winter here is cold; the snow is like a winding sheet—I couldn't bear it!"

She was wavering again; it brought him back, fiery, impatient—

"We will go to Lugano, Italy, Spain; you will get your divorce, I will marry you."

"No! No!—there is no divorce in the Church—I am afraid of Father Cabello."

Those fear thoughts—how they tore at her!

He took her in his arms, kissed her until the color came back to her face, the warmth to her body. She was his absolutely; he could make her do what he wanted—but—he mustn't leave her.

Then she gave a sudden cry. It was like an animal in pain.

"What now? What now?"

"My boy! You won't let them take him away, you must promise me that."

"Julie, look at me."

She raised her heavy lids and met his searching glance; their souls questioned mutely, answered mutely. He drew her closer.

"You shall have your boy. I promise you. Are you satisfied now?"

"Yes—"

She was tired, beaten to exhaustion by the force of rushing psychic waves, breaking against her weak will. Her head throbbed; she tore off her scarf; her hair dropped in a thick coil, down her back, like a writhing white snake; he wound it around his neck.

"This was my punishment."

"No! No! Our love was not a crime. You fought too hard against it. Nature put her hand on your head and turned your hair white; it was her revenge."

Julie listened, fascinated; he was irresistible like that, his voice vibrating. Every nerve in her body responded. He stroked her forehead softly, the pain ceased. How happy she was! how happy.

"You are a woman of the Orient; you are starving for love; it is your life—you cannot fight it; it is too strong for you—for me, come! come!"...

These children of passion went down into the mist.

He carried her along in his strong embrace, lifting her over the stones, her feet scarcely touching the ground; there was a wonderful sense of lightness, as if she had thrown off a heavy load. The fog was cold; it dampened her face, her hair. They reached the bottom of the ravine; the clouds around them moved, disclosing a little wooden house, which had been hidden in the mist. Now it stood out clearly—a bit of beautiful old architecture. Julie shrank away.

"It is a chapel; see, over the door, the cross. Take me home! take me home!"

He laughed mockingly.

"Nonsense, you must get over your religious superstition. The chapel will shelter us from the storm. Come, let us go in."

"No! No!—not there!"

She fled, he followed her; the mist dropped like a curtain between them, growing thicker, thicker.

"Julie, where are you?"

He heard her voice close to him.

"Here."

He took her in his arms, wrapped his cape about her; she clung to him. He was deliriously happy; he held her in a frenzy of possession.

"Julie, my love! my love!"

The mist rose slowly, the red rays of the setting sun penetrated into the ravine, they were enveloped in flames. He could see her face now distinctly as she lay in his arms.

The mist vanished like magic, and—there—there!—he saw—no! no!—it couldn't be!

Floyd's voice rang out through the pass, struck the mountainside, and came back.

"Julie!!"

Martin held her with a fierce joy. He would stand now in the open for what he was. Julie was crying pitifully. He was very tender. He soothed her like a child.

"Hush! Hush! It is better; there will be no more lies."

Floyd's first impulse was to drag her from Martin's arms, but he stood motionless listening to her sobs. Then she tore herself away, with an appealing cry. "Floyd! Forgive me! Forgive me!"

That set both the men on fire. Martin gave an angry growl.

Again Floyd's voice rang out.

"Julie, you are my wife. You must come with me!"

A moment's silence, the trees motionless, the clouds sullen, waiting; then the voice of Nature, so long suppressed, broke out in Julie.

"No! No! I belong to Martin! I will not leave him! I cannot!"

Martin stood a little above her, he put out his hand to draw her up, she smiled at him. God! her joy!

Floyd raised his pistol, fired; Martin's arm fell to his side. Now burning with a murderous rage, he sprang forward at closer range.

"This time through the heart!"

With a cry of horror, Julie wrested the pistol from his hand. It fell some distance away, went off, reverberating through the valley, arousing the people. The pastor heard it in the little chapel, where he had gone at the approach of the storm. He came holding up his lantern, seeking the cause. A fierce gust of wind blew through the ravine, whirling, in a dervish-like dance of fiendish fury.

Then the demon in Martin went out to meet the tearing forces of nature.

"Fool! Fool! You cannot hold her! She was never yours! never! She is mine by Nature's unalterable law!"

Floyd's agonized tones rose above the wind.

"Julie! Julie! I want to save you from a terrible fate! look at him! Can't you see! He is mad! mad!"

That word struck Martin a fatal blow. He put his hand to his head; there was a look in his eyes like a stricken beast pleading for mercy. Floyd never forgot it.

"No! No!—not that—"

He turned and fled, stumbling over rocks, through bushes, a terrible horror pursuing him, stretching out its giant claws to entangle him Mad! Yes, he was mad! It was his inheritance! The storm raged, crashes of thunder, flashes of lightning; an enormous tree sprang into the air, its great quivering limbs cleft in twain. The pines wailed, muttered, waved their long arms; he staggered on, fighting the elements without, within. He was conscious of climbing; his strength grew; fear made him superhuman. He heard a voice behind him calling. Mad! Mad! He went on crashing through obstacles, going up! up— there was no measurement of time, of distance. He stood on the first peak of the great mountain. It rose before him, a straight wall of stone; a deep chasm yawned between. He threw out his arms with agonizing longing.

"Up there! Up to the top!"

There was no trace of mist. The air was cold, the sky studded with brilliant planets; their light searched his soul. He saw clearly the jungle within him, the tearing beasts of passion, the wreckage, the futility, the dark future! He raised his head to that glory once more; then with a cry of despair he went over the precipice.

23

The pastor followed Martin to the foot of the mountain. He could go no further; the ground was slippery, dangerous. He retraced his steps with a heavy heart. He was filled with righteous anger. One of his name had dishonored a woman; he must make restitution. He found Julie in a frenzy of fear, calling again and again, "Martin! Martin!" She stood like a white spirit, erect in the storm. The lightning rent the clouds; then the floods came down.

They carried her to the shelter of the chapel. The little building, centuries old, was originally a storehouse for contraband, a refuge for bandits who hid themselves from the gendarmes, among the wine barrels, in the caves beneath. When the Church took it, they brought a beautiful altar from Italy, and artists who painted religious figures on the walls. The wine caves were partitioned into cells, where pious monks prayed and rubbed their rheumatic limbs. Finally, this holy place, a victim of skeptical times, was used as a theatre, where allegorical plays dealing with the political and religious history of the country were performed.

When Julie became conscious of the dimly lit altar, with its faded velvet and gold lace, its figure of the Virgin in painted wood, she stood transfixed; she saw herself on the day of her confirmation, her mother putting around her neck a gold chain and cross, she heard her own voice repeating the Confession of Faith, the organ pealing the Hymn of Praise, the lights, the Presence! With a cry of anguish she fell on her knees.

"Holy Mary, Mother of God, have pity!"

Then a deep, tender voice filled the chapel—the voice of Father Cabello.

24

Father Cabello was a mystic. Brought up within the walls of a monastery, dedicated to Heaven from his birth, he saw the will of God in every event of his kaleidoscopic existence. He had travelled much, studied much, with the one ever-dominating ambition, which slowly but inevitably came to its fulfillment. The Gonzola family, with money and influence, had in those two generations been a great Catholic influence in America. Father Cabello was the power behind it. He had sustained Mrs. Gonzola, that devout, pious woman, in her awful struggles with Joseph Abravanel. He loved Julie, held himself responsible for her soul. He would save her, as he had saved her mother.

He had been ill in Rome, stricken down with fever, caught in the unsanitary quarters, trying to improve the deplorable condition of the people; he went down under a hopeless task. Many a night, seated at his luxurious table, with its rich appointments, its costly wines, a terrible thought would come again and again: Was the poverty of its children a curse laid upon the Holy City, for the generations of intolerance—its auto-da-fé, its crusades? He tried to drive those haunting spirits away; he was not the Judge, only an insignificant part of an indestructible Institution, a symbol, the moulded image of an Iron Will. Delirium consumed him. He was for weeks near death; then came very slowly back to life. Lying on his flowered terrace, the great panorama of Rome before him, he thought of Julie. She had written to him often after he left America, but her letters grew less frequent. Before his sickness he had received a short note from Mary, telling of Julie's second collapse and her trip to Switzerland: the arsenic waters at the Val Sinestra had helped her wonderfully; the cure would end July twenty-second. There was apparently nothing to cause uneasiness in the letter.

Father Cabello was ostensibly of Jesuit origin, but he possessed a much older secret inheritance from the time when his ancestors were noble Spanish-Maranos, deeply versed in deception and the Talmud. He scented the trail of disaster. Why had not Julie written to him herself? Why had she travelled to Europe without her husband, her child? Why? Why?

The doctors advised him to go on a visit to America, where the climate would drive the malaria out of his system. He refused; his strength was not equal to so long a journey. Then they advised Disentis in Switzerland—one of the few strong-holds left to the Church. He was haunted with the thought of Julie. He would go to the Val Sinestra and see for himself.

Disentis—its crumbling piles of stone, monasteries of the seventh century, its stillness, its health-giving air, the wonderful healing waters, gushing from the earth into natural rock basins, hollowed out by Nature's hand, the frugal fare, the rising at the first glimpse of dawn, the pervading sweetness of the bells, prayer, which had a new sanctity, as if nearer the Divine Fount—there he gained new spiritual inspiration, new physical strength—there during the summer months the Benedictine Friars welcome their brothers from all corners of the world. Father Cabello clasped hands with monks of many orders. The Trappists appealed strongly to his affection—bare-footed, humble, rich in knowledge; he never tired listening to their many colored experiences. He was eagerly questioned about America, "the land of unbounded possibilities." He had a store of humorous stories, which were greeted with low chuckles and spasmodic movements of the diaphragm.

Walking with the Father Superior one day, in the surrounding woods, that benign forest which protects the children of God from the avalanche, Father Cabello asked about Val Sinestra and how he could get there.

"Easily from here; my carriage is at your disposal—a drive at leisure through the mountains, a most beautiful and interesting trip. Near the Val Sinestra, there is an ancient bit of architecture, a deserted chapel; it is now the property of a poor community headed by a great man, Pastor Staehli; the Church should buy it back."

"I will see to it," said Father Cabello.

The next day he started out; there was no trace of anger in the blue sky, but the driver pointed to a small watery cloud low on the horizon.

"We are going to have a storm; would it not be better to wait until it is over?" said the Superior.

Father Cabello hesitated, then he answered:

"I want to be at Val Sinestra before the twenty-second. I am being pushed by a strong impulse, which has some mysterious significance—a call for help from one I love."

"Then go, in God's name."

That drive through the mountains was a sacrament. Father Cabello bowed before a great God, clothed in a sacerdotal vestment of Nature.

"There is the chapel," said the driver. It was distinctly visible in the valley below.

Suddenly a shot rang out.

"What was that?"

The driver shook his head. It seemed to the excited imagination of the priest like a discharge signalling a great battle; then the fury of the Invisible broke, the man whipped up his horses, and dashed down the incline toward the chapel....

It is wonderful in the mountains after such an outbreak of electric force; the Prince of Light marches majestically in the Heavens showering gifts of prismatic gold; a Master Chemist, he will create again from the storm wreckage; the stricken trees will sink into the bosom of the earth and moulder there, generating in Nature's crucible new germs of Life, and the little dark pine-children will be born.

25

Floyd paced restlessly outside the chapel, listening to Julie's sobs and the voice of the priest, tender, persuasive, stern, threatening. Once before he had pleaded with Joseph Abravanel; now a second time he is pleading with his wife! His wife? No! No! Lies! Lies! She was never his; she belonged to Martin by the unalterable law of Nature. They would go on saying that. He would always see them with their arms around each other. He had been cheated! cheated!

A sharp bolt of light pierced the dark valley, shone on the battered cross above the chapel, glanced off, lit up the silver trimmings of the pistol on the ground. He picked it up. The voices in the chapel rose and fell.

"You must go back to your husband."

"I will not. I belong to Martin; I will never leave him. I cannot." Her voice was sharp with agony. Floyd shuddered; why should she be tortured like that? Why? If he were dead they could live. He *was* dead, burnt to cinders. The tongues of flame in his father's workshop had crept into his body, consumed it; there was nothing left but the shell—easy enough to put an end to that clay image!—"Shoot its head off!"

The pastor wrested the pistol from the hand of the distraught man, led him through a trail to the châlet, and left him with Angela. He was quiet now; he lay back in a chair with closed eyes. She sat and watched him, passing her cool hand over his hot forehead; the lamp shed a soft glow over the pale face, the well-shaped head, the regular features. A splendid human species, those Americans—a youthful race, a type ennobled by climate, good food, and labor that develops character. She thought of the cretins of her own beautiful land, of the degenerating races of Europe. This man was like Dresden china, fine, very fine; but there were deep lines that made the face look old; the chisel of Life had cut deeply into him. She bent over him.

"Come with me."

He looked blankly into her soft radiant eyes. Who was she?

She took him up the narrow stairs into a small room with bare white walls, a little cot, a bunch of Alpine roses on a table by the window.

"Will you try to sleep?"

"No! No!"

She led him to the balcony, a nest under the overhanging roof.

"Sit here; you will sleep."

She put him in a reclining chair and left him.

The moon shone on his flushed face; the valley was filled with soft shadows; the mountain raised a luminous head. The air penetrated his agonized body. An hour passed; a white figure stood beside him.

"Come in! The night air in the mountains is too strong for strangers."

He saw her through a mist, his eyes dim with overpowering sleep. He fell on the cot—she covered him with a warm blanket....

The pastor called the guides together; they came with their ropes and axes. He spoke tersely; they were used to action, not words.

"A man had gone up the mountain in the storm."

Then he gave a low whistle. There was a panting, a breaking through the bushes. A dog threw himself upon the pastor, who bent over him, stroking his thick coat with a magnetic touch. He gave him Martin's mantle, the dog tore at it, dropped it. The pastor whispered, "Find him." With a low whine the animal plunged into the thicket, the guides followed, their strong throats propelling sounds that echoed to the unscaled heights.

26

The hotel was in an uproar. The pale women, excited by the storm, could not be kept in their rooms; they crowded the corridors, uttering plaintive cries. The quick flashes of lightning revealed little groups huddled together; one poor thing quite lost her control. She betrayed her terror in a strangely interesting manner: rushed to the long door opening onto the balcony, baring her white bosom to the storm. She was wonderful as she stood there, her face rapturous, like a woman lifting herself to the embrace of her lover.

The storm passed. The pale women fluttered in the sun, holding up their bloodless hands to its warmth, chattering, laughing over their "thrilling" experience.

Mary was terribly worried about her friends. The carriage had not come back. The proprietress thought the party had been driven through the short cut to the pastor's châlet.

"But the shot!" said Mary. The woman looked grave. It was not hunting time.

When the carriage drove up with Julie and Father Cabello, Mary knew something terrible had happened. She grew very pale, but she had been trained to ask no questions. Julie was quiet, with wide-open horror-filled eyes. Father Cabello took Mary's hand and spoke gravely.

"There has been an accident. Mr. Steele has been lost in the storm; they are looking for him." She caught her breath.

"Mr. Garrison?"

The priest pierced her with his understanding eyes.

"Mr. Garrison is safe; he and his wife will leave here by the early train tomorrow. Will you see to everything?"

"Yes," said Mary.

Then his voice hardened.

"No matter what happens, they must go; nothing can prevent that."

Julie let herself be undressed and fell into a lethargy. Mary tried several times to awaken her; she would open her eyes and fall again into that trance which was not sleep.

The pastor came over to the hotel to see Father Cabello. They talked long into the night, of Floyd, Julie, of the fight against Martin. The pastor repeated again:

"He is one of ours; he has done wrong. He must make restitution."

Father Cabello was troubled. Julie had shown unexpected strength. He must find a way to bring her back to the Church, to submission.

The next morning, early, Mary was surprised to find Julie up and dressed. The hotel was closing that day. The trunks had to be locked and taken down. Julie watched her moving about.

"If I could get out of this room—it is horrible."

A hotel room before the departure of its occupant, with its torn newspapers, remnants of food, bedclothes thrown in a heap—there is nothing more desolate, more inexpressibly forlorn.

They went down to an empty room on the ground floor, misnamed the "children's playroom." The pale women were unmarried or childless. Julie moved continually from one window to another; when she saw Father Cabello and Floyd coming up the walk, she shrank into a corner, a terrified hunted thing.

Father Cabello found Floyd very quiet; whatever may have been his feelings, he had them under perfect control. He answered the priest's questions in as few words as possible, and listened without comment to his sophistical justification of Julie.

"Perhaps your wife was not all to blame."

"Perhaps not."

"You know Julie's nature—she is easily influenced."

"Yes, I know."

"The man must have persecuted her."

"Perhaps he did."

"I don't wish to blame *you*, but knowing what has happened and the desperate character of the man, was it right to let your wife travel alone?"

"Perhaps it was not right. But it didn't occur to me."

When they entered the room, Floyd stood quietly at the door. The priest went to Julie and took her hand.

"Julie, you must ask your husband to forgive you."

The answer came again:

"I will not. I belong to Martin; I will never leave him!"

The priest's wrath was terrible. He stormed, threatened, pleaded—she must go with her husband; there must be no scandal. She must go home to her child.

Floyd was white to the lips—Mary couldn't bear it. She rushed out of the room....

The pastor came up the terrace; Father Cabello went out to meet him and brought him in. He spoke quietly, with deep feeling.

"The guides who were seeking Martin Steele have come down from the mountain."

"Have they found him?"

"Yes. He is dead."

There was a silence. It was Floyd this time who cried with a rush of repentant agony:

"Martin! I killed him! I am a murderer!"

"No! he himself was responsible. He met the fate of the rash. A man must know the precipices and how to avoid them before he tries to climb."

Again came the cry from Floyd:

"I shot to kill! I shot to kill!"

"The guides followed his traces up the mountain; there were signs that told a human thing had passed. He must have gone over at the first plateau. They went down as far as they dared. There were broken branches; the violence of the fall tore up a young tree with its roots. Come with me, I will show you where he struck the trail. There was madness upon him, his senses wandered, the inevitable happened."

They stood in the quiet woods and looked up at the wall of stone where Martin had said, "I will climb that mountain."

The pastor put his arm around Floyd.

"My son, you have been through more than your share of trouble; don't burden yourself with morbid self accusations. He was your friend; he betrayed you. He made the only reparation—death. Try to think kindly of him. Under natural conditions he would have been a brave son of the soil. He was robbed of his birthright...."

Julie shed no tears. The old fear was upon her; the Punishment had come again in the shape of Death, and *he* had paid. The priest worked upon this superstitious dread; it was the only way to subdue her. "God had punished her for her crime against her husband. He would punish her further; she must go home, she must go back to her religion, God had struck Martin with the whip of retribution. He would bring it down upon her shoulders if she did not repent. A great calamity would happen to her child."

She was cowed, humble, on her knees before him begging for mercy. He confessed her, and gave her absolution.

Mr. and Mrs. Garrison left by the afternoon train; they were a pitiable sight, these two unhappy children wondering why the world was so dark, the pain so hard to bear. The priest spoke the last words.

"My children, you are going home. You will be happy again, if you do not nourish your misfortune. God has given us the magic of memory, and a still greater blessing, the gift of forgetting."

They bowed their heads to his blessing. The train left the station, wending its way in and out of the tunnels.

"When I watch those undulations," said the pastor to Father Cabello, "I think of a serpent crawling into the great centers of vice, carrying with him the modern Adams, the curious Eves, who will eat copiously of the fruit of the Tree of Knowledge."

The priest smiled. The simile appealed to his mind trained in Biblical metaphors.

"I have no fears for our young couple; the New World moulds its people. The practical life of which they are an integral part will make their road clear to them. I have lived long in America. It is a land of proof, not belief; of practical results and a kind of idealism which is expressed in action. There is no time for dreams; inspiration feeds only on quick realization. A land of no secrets, where publicity methods are applied alike to business, science, literature, religion. That which cannot be exploited is called 'high-brow'— but there is a saving humor in it all. America is a great country."

The pastor answered with just a touch of good-natured satire.

"If there are no secrets, how is it that the Church has prospered there?"

The priest smiled enigmatically.

"The Church adapts itself....

"I am going back to Rome, with a mind at rest. We have held together the thread of two lives which threatened to snap, nay, three lives: there is a boy whose career must be watched closely. Other forces are at work—race impulses; they must be eradicated."

"Is that possible?"

"Yes, but difficult. I shall bring the boy to Rome; there, all other influences will be neutralized."

The pastor offered his hospitality for the night, which was gratefully accepted. It had been a turbulent time ending happily. The priest was in a frame of mind harmonizing with the beauty of approaching twilight. They sat outside the châlet. The pastor filled long glasses with the wine of the Canton, which expands the Soul. They sat there, looking into the Val Sinestra, until the sun scattered rubies and the moon threw down a silver veil.

They talked of the future of religion and the wave of unbelief sweeping over the world.

"When I meet a man like you," said the priest, "I regret the loss to the Church. Protestantism was at best a frail child; it cannot survive without support. Why should it not come back? We would kill the fatted calf to celebrate the return of our Prodigal Son."

The pastor saved the situation with a fine sense of humor.

"My friend, we are not father and son: we are brothers, prodigal children of the great original God of the Hebrews."

The priest's eyes gleamed.

"Then why not a family reunion? It has been my life's dream—all sects united in the spacious bosom of the true Faith."

The pastor nodded in silent approval. Then Luther would come into his own. At this same moment, far away in the East, the muezzin was chanting from the minarets, calling the people to prayer. "There is but one God, and Mohammed is his Prophet," and at this same time, millions of humans, prostrate before Buddha, were praying to attain the perfection of the Soul—Nirvana; and the "chosen people" once again in Jerusalem were praising the "only" God, who had led them out of exile into the land of their fathers. The priest and the pastor would soon solve their problem—they were both approaching with silent rapid steps, the solution of the Great Mystery.

The next morning Father Cabello thanked the pastor again for his good offices. He was a practical man, and in the light of day, dreams evaporate. He did not speak of buying the chapel; he wanted to go in peace.

27

Angela sat at the wheel, her quick skilful fingers spinning the yellow thread. The girl, with her unerring instinct of the unseen, felt the air weighing heavily. The atmosphere of the house was charged with sadness; unhappy spirits had passed through, leaving something of their sorrow, their passions. The anguish of Floyd still lingering in her little room kept her awake at night. The dead man was always before her—his uneven gait, the passionate face, the glittering eyes. A great longing went out from her to that rebellious soul, beating so long against bars, a prisoner in his own body....

The pastor had gone over to the hotel for Martin's one valise and the little deerskin box. He spoke to the woman of the house; she remembered her father telling of a Staehli who went "across seas" and never came back. The crooked gardener, shuffling about, chimed in.

"Yes, I knew Martin Staehli. He had a quarrel with a guide about a woman, and shot him dead. He was hot blooded."

"The man lost on the mountain was his grandson," said the pastor.

"Strange things happen in a lifetime," mumbled the gardener. "Now who would believe, to look at me, that I was once the champion wrestler of the village!"...

The next morning at sunrise the pastor knocked at Angela's door.

"Angela, we are going 'up there' today."

During the summer, when they were pasturing the cattle, she and the pastor spent many a happy time with the peasant boys and girls who had gone up in June, clinging gradually from one plateau to another until they reached the top, where they would stay until the weather drove them down.

Angela sprang joyfully out of bed and went to fetch her basket; on the way up she would look for herbs. It was wonderful how she spied the rare plants hid away under the rocks and at the bottom of brooks. They went slowly, at first, Angela timing her steps to the pastor's, who grasped his stick, gaining strength as he climbed. Not far behind, a guide followed, carrying the belongings of the unfortunate man. In Switzerland every waterfall, river, flower, bush, and tree has its legendary Spirit. Miracle stories come down by word of mouth. The old grandmother sitting outside the châlet at night, a pipe between her toothless gums, her needle running a race with her tongue, tells the children of the wonders of the mountains:

"In the old days, when a mountaineer had been lost on the heights, the peasants would go from peak to peak calling his name. Where the echo repeated they stopped, and would throw down articles of clothing and a large cheese from the milk of the missing man's herd, to keep his spirit from cold and starvation. They tell of a peasant who was lost. They let down his dog on a rope. The faithful animal, whining in low dog tones, eagerly scented the way. When they drew up the rope it was bitten through. The dog had found the body of his master and would not leave him. Whenever there is a thick mist the peasant is seen, his dog beside him, on the edge of the chasm, pointing with a warning finger to the precipice."...

The merry band of dairy workers welcomed the pastor with shrill cries and clarion notes from Alpine horns. It was a modest community; each one owned his little herd. There were many huts, where the milk is set in earthen bowls, yielding cream, butter, cheese, their only wealth. The pastor drew a herdsman aside and spoke to him in low tones. A stillness fell on the merry band. The man led them across the field to a deep pool fed by mountain torrents; at a narrow end was a rough rustic bridge, which they crossed in single file, and came into a thick pine grove. Farther on, the clearing was carpeted with roses, anemones, violets. They walked carefully, not to crush them; then they climbed up a steep rock to a cow-hut on the top.

Angela gave a low cry. A man lay on a bed of hay, his arm in a rough splinter, his face the wax of death. She dropped down beside him, listened to his heart, tried to raise his closed lids.

"He is dead."

"I think not," answered the peasant. "I have seen many such cases of suspended animation, from the shock of a heavy fall."

Then he told them how Martin had been saved from going to the bottom of the precipice by being caught in a crevice of the rocks. He was found tightly wedged in, covered by the stones that had rolled down. The dog had scented the place where he lay. It would be a miracle if he lived.

The pastor patted the head of the animal, who would now and again put his paw very gently on the man's chest, as if seeking for heart-beats. Then he'd lick the white face, wag his tail, and stretch himself out again.

"I won't give up hope," said the pastor, "until the dog howls and slinks away."

Angela was moving about. She made a wood fire on the rock outside, filled a large iron pot with water, and stirred in her herbs with which she would bathe his bruised body. They emitted a pungent, agreeable perfume. The pastor watched her as she stood, a bright figure against the dark pine background: "a blessed child."

Angela passed the night in a hut with the dairy maids. She was intensely awake, concentrating her entire spiritual power. She ceased to be a human thing; she became a Thought, a disembodied Will. She arose from the bed where the peasant girls were sleeping, three together, their arms entwined, their hair sweeping the ground, their white arms and bosoms like ivory in the night light—a great picture of future mothers, bearing in their bodies the next generation. She stepped out into the air, listened to the walking of the waters, the talking of the trees; she heard panting. Something warm pressed against her. The dog jumped on her, whining. What was the message? Was it death? She followed the excited animal over the stones, over the pool, into the hut. The man was lying as she had left him, but there was something in his face that made her heart leap. She took the limp form in her arms. The breath of her young body, the life that was in the sap of the trees, the minerals of the springs, the healing balsam of the air, all the natural force in her, and more, the dynamic power of the spirit, went out to him. Her hands, tingling with electricity, moved tensely over his chest, his limbs; the dog watched, helping with his mute soul. Suddenly the curtains over the heavy eyes quivered, opened, then dropped again; her fingers on his pulse felt slow intermittent throbs. She had dragged him from the depths—he hovered for weeks between Life and the Beyond, coming back slowly, but the mind remained inert. The summer was unusually mild; they put him outside on a soft bed of boughs, where he lay day and night in silence with the dog beside him, his eyes following Angela as she moved about. She taught him to walk again, guiding his steps carefully.

The pastor came weekly to see him, spoke to him, but he didn't answer. Angela grew anxious.

"Does he think?"

"I believe not," said the pastor. "It is a kind of aphasia, which time will cure."

Angela wondered if he could distinguish sounds—the chirping of the birds, the bark of the dog, the music of the herd. The peasants would tell in lowered voices of a shadow of a man standing under the pines, so still, the chamois would come closer, closer, looking at him with their soft, beseeching eyes; then they'd scamper away....

August!—It was bleak. The man sat on the trunk of a tree; he was without the thrill of life.

The pastor spoke to him.

"Do you want anything?"

"No."

"Do you know me?"

A flash passed over the face.

"Yes."

The pastor's voice grew stern.

"You will go down tomorrow with the herdsmen. You are the peasant Staehli: they are your people; you are one of them. You have been all your life in exile; now you are on your natural soil. The voice of race will awaken in you—you will find yourself."

The man listened, agonized with the intensity of concentration; the words cut like sharp stones into him.

"You understand, you are the peasant Staehli."

The answer came back mechanically:

"I am the peasant Staehli."

The next day, Staehli the peasant went down with the herds from plateau to plateau, lingering while the weather favored. Late in the summer they reached the valley.

28

Winter in that little hidden-away corner of the world, snow without beginning, without end, scarcity of food, dread of the avalanche. The peasant is a fatalist, accepting the inevitable with silence, with awe. "God is good; He sends summer as a rich reward."

The pastor shared the hard lot of his parish. The Devil was always there in the shape of "schnaaps," driving the simple souls to madness, making cretins of their children. The pastor fought the "Evil One" with holy ire like his great ancestor Martin Luther. Every night he would take his lantern and tramp over to the Inn, sit with "his children," drink with them moderately, see the liquor locked up, put the key in his pocket, and go his way. Many a morning he found the cupboard tampered with, pretending not to see the lock had been repaired. Now Martin went with him, sitting silent, answering laconically.

The pastor gave him much physical labor—washed out roads to remake, wood to cut and draw. There was a landslide; a part of the village was under snow. Martin worked with pick and shovel to dig out the people, carrying the women and children in his arms, his strength growing as the hardiest collapsed. When it was too cold for the old man, Martin went alone to the Inn to lock up.

One night, walking home, the sky like velvet studded with clustered diamonds, the mysterious blue light on the snow, the silence, the penetrating beauty, threw a spell over him. He wandered till the unseen sun shot up faint rays, turning the white world into faded rose; then memory stirred in him. Angela saw him tracing with a piece of charcoal on a board. She put slips of paper and pencil in his way; he scribbled on them, threw them down, forgot them. They were confused lines crossing, recrossing, impressionist shapes of mountains, and always the faint outlines of a woman's head. She put them carefully in a box he would remember some day. She saw quick flashes in his eyes, sparks blazing up, dying out.

He sat outside the châlet, hammering nails into the soles of the mountain boots he had made for himself. The Staehlis had always learnt a trade—they were shoemakers, tanners, blacksmiths, herders, sons of toil and of the soil. The pastor stood watching him.

"The snow has melted in the valley, the sky is clear. We will wander forth— to the south first, and back on foot when the trees blossom."

They started off in the early morning. An old peasant, leaning somewhat heavily on his solid staff of hickory wood, a young peasant, silent, unsmiling. Angela put paper and crayon in his knapsack.

"Bring me pictures; they tell more than words."

They tramped through valleys, over hills, jumping on hay-wagons, climbing into stage-coaches, riding the sure-footed mountain pony. The pastor watched Martin. There were blood streaks in his eyes; his face was like a wax mask.

They came to lovely Lugano, the Fatima in Switzerland's harem of beauties, warm, passionate—the soft Italian patois, Italian air, Italian skies.

"Over there across the lake is Milan, Rome, the Raphael frescoes."

Martin's eyes gleamed; then he shook his head. The pastor sighed—would he ever wake up?

Geneva—intellectual, proud of its men of genius. They walked through Rousseau's Island of Exile.

"He was greatly gifted," said the pastor, "but the victim of his own sensuality."

"We are all that," said Martin. Then the veil of melancholy dropped again.

"When we are conscious of it, the cure is there. Rousseau was the mind of his generation; he might have been its soul, but he never found himself."

Einsiedeln—with its monasteries a thousand years old, its few sad Benedictine hermits poring over their ancient manuscripts, restoring the eaten-away remnants, kept with pious reverence hidden in old chests. Einsiedeln—its pilgrims, its Life Eternal, hypnotized, under the spell of religion.

Arosa—the bleak mountains, the hopeless sick wrapped in blankets on open balconies. Martin shivered.

"Let us go."

Zurich again, with its historical surroundings. The pastor told the story of Charlemagne who, finding a toad sitting in the nest of a beautiful serpent, drove it out and killed it with one blow of his heavy stick. "There was a banquet at the Palace that night; the guards were terrified at the sight of a white spotted snake who crawled into the hall, wound herself up on the legs of a chair, and dropped a priceless jewel into the goblet of wine which the monarch held to his lips, giving him the magic gift of compelling the love of all who set eyes on him."

"A toad in her nest," repeated Martin....

Two months in the cities, then the country beautiful—the trees heavy with white blossoms, bearing embryonic fruit. Toward evening the air grew heavy with the day's perfume; the night was warm in the valley. Martin moved about restlessly.

"I cannot sleep; let us go into the woods."

They walked through dark trails, lit faintly by stars shining through the trees; then he broke a long silence, speaking of himself for the first time, slowly, timidly.

"The air goes through me; it is sweeping away that terrible fear. If I could be free of the horror that tears at me, the horror of—madness."

The pastor spoke eagerly.

"Fight it, Martin, drive it out. It is an illusion, an evil thought that does not exist. Martin, your soul is in prison, beating its wings against the bars of your own obstinacy; let it soar."

"I cannot. I am choked with wild impulses, driving me to distraction. I am mad! I tell you, mad!"

"Martin! there is a madness which destroys, and a madness that reveals; such madness has been the salvation of the world. Come, sit down with me, here in this forest, where once lived and suffered our great ancestor, our patron Saint, Mad Martin."

"Mad Martin?"

Then he told in picturesque English, lapsing unconsciously into his own musical Romansch, the legend of Mad Martin.

"He was one of a lawless band, the youngest bandit of them all—a beautiful youth with the grace of a wild stag, without fear or sense of right, prowling about with his carbine, robbing, killing, consorting with lewd women. One night, a night like this in the woods where holiness dwelt, something stirred within him—a voice clear, beautiful, said wonderful things which gave his soul wings."

"Yes! that happens sometimes, a voice from within," said Martin.

"He left the band, made his way to the church and begged to be taken in. He was rarely gifted; the monks saw in him the white fervor of the saint. The Lord had changed the murderous rage of the robber into the divine madness of the fanatic. He went to Einsiedeln and there, it was said, heard the voice of God, who commanded him to become a monk. As the story goes, the Lord, to try his piety, put in his way a last temptation. He was walking in the woods, reading his prayers, when he suddenly came upon a beautiful vicious thing who had loved him in his bandit days; she put her arms around him, her mouth to his. He forgot Heaven. He tried to tear himself away. Her kisses held him. She lured him to her cabin and in the intoxication of passion, he took no count of time."

"Her kisses held him," repeated Martin.

"She made a plan that would bind him to her forever; she plied him with wine until his senses fled, stripped him naked, crowned him with a wreath of red poppies, left him dancing and singing ribald songs, a young Bacchus in the woods; then she called the priests to witness his degradation. They believed her not; the young Divine was deep in the under cells, fasting, praying, purifying his body, preparing for his ordination. She mocked at them.

"'Fools! He is no priest, he is Mad Martin. He cannot change; his blood still riots in him, calling for wine, for women. If I lie, burn me at the stake!'

"Mad Martin in the woods heard the angry voices of the people, the mocking gibes of the woman, and realized his degradation. He fled to the cabin, locked himself in, fell on his knees, and prayed for help. The chanting of priests, the cries of the people grew louder—their axes were breaking down the door. The poor sinner raised his arms to Heaven, with a cry, in which his battered, stricken soul took joyful flight. When the enraged people burst into the cabin, they found it empty. They searched the cells of the monastery; there was no trace of him. The Father Superior, a holy man of years, was calm.

"'Wait, he will not fail us.'

"The day of consecration came; among the young priests stood a tall figure in white, ready to take his vows. He was pale and faint from fasting, but his voice was like a bell sounding from the distance. As he left the altar there was a bright light on his face. The people followed him on their knees. He put out his hands, blessed them, and the cripples threw away their crutches and the sick were well. Then he blessed Einsiedeln and made it a holy place for pilgrims in the ages to come. He blessed the village under the mountain, where he was born, sinned, and atoned, and prophesied its future peace, prosperity. Then he disappeared before their eyes, but he has been kept alive in our hearts and memory. Every three years, the people of our village give in the little chapel 'The Miracle of Saint Martin.'"

There was a long silence. Martin sat, his face buried in his hands. The pastor spoke again.

"Martin! Free yourself of this horror; let Hope in. Life is knocking at your door with gifts of fulfillment!"

Martin struggled with the torrent of feeling rushing through him; then the dry eyes grew moist, the tears came. The fever of hate, the passion of Love, the terrible impulse of self destruction, a devil tempting in the night, the thought of life with reason gone—all the dangers of an overwrought mind were washed away in those tears. He dropped down, broken, helpless, on the new sweet hay in a little hut near by; the cool air swept over him. A bird's plaintive call startled the silence—an unforgettable night of spiritual revelation, Peace....

It was dawn when he awoke. He looked about for the Pastor, found him lying in a corner, his mantle wrapped about him. Martin looked long at the noble snow-crowned head, then stole softly out, came upon a clear pool hidden in the trees—we meet them unexpectedly in Switzerland, startling us with their limpid loveliness.

There was a flash of Glory!—the Sun! He felt a sense of elation, of new birth. The sky turned purple, pink, gold; the color ecstasy crept into his blood. Color! the life of the world! Color clamored in his brain for expression, for air; he was obsessed with the madness that reveals, the divine madness of the artist.

The pastor stood beside him. The sun was climbing. Martin pointed to a ball of fire down deep in the lake.

"I'm going to bring it up," he said. He slipped off his clothes and dived in, floating, twisting himself like a dolphin, spouting water in the air; then he ran along the green borders, his body gleaming in the sun. The pastor thought of the legend of the Water Gods.

They went slowly on foot toward home, stopping at the little Dorfs, where the peasants greeted them with acclamations. "A fine lad! a Staehli, every inch of him." Martin returned their gripping handshakes, tossed down their schnaaps, gave them points on the disinfection of barns and the care of cows, danced with the maids on the green, kissed them; they pelted him with flowers.

At the door of the châlet, Angela stood waiting. He put a portfolio in her hands, bits of color he had caught on the way. Her eyes were fixed on his face. This was not the Martin she had known: it was like the same face reflected in clear water, etherealized by the refraction of light. She heard him in the fields, his strong voice filling the distance with melody. She looked up at the great mountain. An unfortunate man called Martin Steele lay there, dead.

29

The Garrisons came back to their home on Park Avenue. With Mary's help and his own will, Floyd learnt to diagnose Julie's actions as "psychic impulses." She herself couldn't do wrong; she fought against a "subconscious tendency." From her girlhood it had always been "like that"; this was the bridge over which he could pass to reconciliation. He had every reason to be satisfied with his wife. She was in correspondence with Father Cabello, whose influence revealed itself in her piety. She became very devout, Heavenly love drove out the earthly in her. She attended daily mass; the big-eyed woman with her beautiful boy were well-known at the Cathedral. Floyd noticed after coming home from service a rapt expression on her face; she went about with upturned eyes like St. Cecilia. He had a vision of a black-robed nun. He spoke to Dr. McClaren.

"I am afraid my wife is developing a religious complex."

"I think not," answered the doctor. "I imagine before it gets so far, that insatiable emotional craving of hers will find a new stimulus."

There was something wrong with Floyd. His intense desire to forget the "unpleasant" episode in Switzerland had overstrained his nerves. They reacted in a strange manner. He'd leave his home in the morning with the intention of going to see the Colonel, and would find himself wandering aimlessly in quite a different direction. He'd walk for hours through parts of the city unknown to him; he saw strange faces, strange places, another world. He lounged about where the ships came in. The immigrants had an irresistible fascination. He watched them, listened to their unintelligible jargon. A dark-eyed Madonna with a shawl on her head, a child at her breast, was not strange to him. He knew her: she was Julie's sister. A bearded old man, carrying on his bent shoulders the tragedy of his race, looked at him with the eyes of Joseph Abravanel. A straight tall peasant with bundles, bewildered by the city, was Martin's grandfather. It was a kind of mental phantasmagoria of those who had worked a sinister influence in his life. He couldn't get rid of them; he saw their Past, their Present, their Future, the struggles, the agony, the hopelessness. He was flung backward, forward with them. Must he go on living with them all his life? A horror seized him.

"Taxi, sir, take you anywhere—"

A tall chauffeur with dark goggles took him by the arm and lifted him into the cab.

"Where to, sir?"

Floyd bent forward, he knew that voice.

"Tom Dillon!"

"Mr. Garrison. You won't say anything."

Floyd grasped his hand with quick sympathy and drew him into the car. Tom choked at first, but gradually recovering himself, told his story.

"I married Maudy, because I couldn't get her any other way. Oh, she was a kisser. She'd go as far as the fence, but she wouldn't jump it. We were coming home from a dance up the road. I tried it on. 'Tom,' she said, 'if you want me, you'll have to marry me.' I married her. I didn't take it seriously. I thought this way: It's as broad as it's long. When I get enough, there's Reno. She flung the dough like Hell; I couldn't see any value for it, only a heap of rags. Anyhow, a man can get liquor and women—"

"Yes, I know."

Tom shifted uneasily in his seat.

"When you don't earn, money melts. My credit kept me going for a time. Then I had to tell her. I was sure she'd leave me. I'm only good to hand out. She told me that lots of times."

"She left you?"

Tom's eyes snapped; he was radiant with pride.

"She didn't. She had an auction sale. All her friends were there; they wouldn't miss it. She sold everything, even her engagement ring, and paid every cent I owed. By God! she did." There was a choked sob. "I had to do something to get even, didn't I?"

"Yes, Tom." Floyd was beginning to respect him.

"I went to my friends, but they wanted solid men in their business, and I couldn't blame 'em. I walked about like a crazy man, couldn't get a job. She kept enough to furnish a band-box in the Bronx. She does all the work. You must see her. She's as pretty as a peach, and the place is as neat as wax."

"But how did you come to this, Tom?"

"She sent me to sell the car; that hurt me. I went and sat around the garage with the boys. I was down and out; they had money to burn. They said, 'Sell? nothing doing—a car like yours is capital.' Well, I didn't sell; I commenced going out nights. I was ashamed to be seen, but I got over that. Then I risked it in the daytime; now I flaunt my shame. I tell you! it's a rotten world—when I had money it was a stunt to do my own repairs. When I took the crowd out joy riding, I was a good sport, but to 'hack' for a living is common. I'm done with that swell bunch. Maudy says they're beneath us."

Then he sat looking at Floyd, his eyes begging.

"Tom, you've solved your problem, I'm proud of you."

Tom heaved a sigh of relief and got back to business.

"Now I suppose you want to get home."

"I don't know," said Floyd, wearily.

Tom gave him a sharp look.

"What are you doing down here anyhow, seeing some capitalist off?"

"No, watching poor wretches come in. I've been through a lot, and I haven't quite got my bearings."

Tom asked no questions, but he told Maudy afterwards he was sure Garrison "had some trouble with that crazy wife of his."

"You'd better come outside with me and get some fresh air—you don't mind me taking a fare if it comes my way. I've got another car; there's a guy in with me. I dope it out this way: he gets twenty-five per cent of the takings, I get the rest and pay for the damn gas. The car's on instalment; when we pay it off we'll go it equal. Fair enough, isn't it?"

"Yes, it is."

Tom had coarsened; the veneer of wealth was gone. Floyd liked him that way.

"You've grown stouter, Tom; you're the picture of health."

Tom, slapping his chest complacently, came in collision with an enormous truck. He let out a stream of oaths, which paralyzed the physically inferior opponent. The poor devil cranked frantically and got out of his way.

"It was your fault, Tom, not his."

"Of course it was, but that alien wouldn't dare open his mouth to a free-born American. If he tried it on, they'd wipe him out."

Tom spoke with a rich Irish inherited brogue, which all his college education hadn't eradicated.

"We were talking about me, weren't we?"

"Yes."

"I've gained thirty pounds, I eat like a hog, and I'm for Prohibition every time. At first I worried myself to bones about Maudy. I was afraid to tell her I was hacking. Her family's a hundred per cent American and she's damn proud. When I brought home money she wouldn't take it—'You're on the crook, Tom, and I'm going to leave you.' Then I blurted it all out. I was frightened stiff—what do you think she did?"

"Haven't any idea, Tom—abused you roundly for a piker?"

"Na—she just hugged me till I didn't have a breath left. 'Tom,' she said, 'I've cried many a long night. I couldn't see *you* making a living. God is good; He wouldn't let me go begging to my rich friends. Hacking's a fine business, but there's something against it—those flappers. Don't take 'em in your car; sooner lose a fare. You're good looking and they'll get you.'"

Floyd laughed. Tom was the right medicine for him.

They were driving uptown—Tom's tongue went faster than the car; he had acquired a lot of practical information. "They're starring the crime wave now, all bunk—we're no worse than we were. Wait till after the election, the prisons will be so empty they'll have to turn 'em into meeting houses. What do you think of them stinking Republicans up in Washington?"

"Tom, don't insult my inherited political party. I've had them handed down to me, and I must carry them."

Tom opened his mouth, the brimstone flowed, the air was blue; then suddenly he was dazzled by two shapely legs encased in flesh-colored cobwebs, and a pair of bright eyes emitting sparks.

"Taxi, Miss?" He drew up to the curbstone, smiling at her, showing his white teeth, sprang out, opened the door, dusted off the seat, held the rug in his hand.

She was undecided. "I don't want to go, yet...."

"Yes you do, but you don't know it," laughed Tom.

A gust of cold wind blew her against him. Tom glanced downward.

"Your legs are cold?"

"Oh! Warm as toast."

"Your blood keeps them warm."

She twisted her little mouth.

"No, my vanity."

Clever girl. Tom lifted her bodily into the car; they were old friends now. He wrapped her in the warm rug and put a match to her cigarette.

"Who's the melancholy Dane in front?"

"Oh! He's a guy I'm breaking in."

They drove to Madison Avenue. She jumped out and gave him a generous fare.

"I want to go out again tonight; call for me?"

He smiled into the pretty laughing eyes. "Awful sorry, Miss, but there's nothing doing. I'm married." He heaved a big sigh.

"She was nice—wasn't she."

Floyd slapped him on the back. "You're a hero, Tom. It was a great temptation." Tom beamed.

"They've taken it into their pretty heads to star the chauffeur. We're the cowboys of the East. We drive and slash about, and lasso them in. Say, I'm afraid I'm going to lose my man—handsome lad, good family. There's a little snipe baiting for him, and she'll hook him too."

At the garage he found a note.

Married this morning to Ida, family approve.

Tom's sorrow was pathetic. "They're rich brokers. They'll put him on the street. He'll never be able to earn an honest penny again. Where shall I find another like him? The girls fell for him every time. He was a handsome fish. You've got nothing to do; help me out just for today. You can run a car. It doesn't need so much experience, and I can't afford to let her stand idle."

"I haven't got the experience, Tom, but I can hand you the good looks," said Floyd, modestly.

Tom was jubilant; he'd have to keep his mind on the wheel—and a few knocks would shake him up.

"Now I'll give you the fruits of my experience. Before you turn a corner, blow the horn, then stop and listen. Don't try to pass anything; let the other fellow smash you up—then you'll get damages. The wise guy says, 'we've got a third eye in the back of our heads.' Exercise yours; it'll work after a while. When an old woman or a cat gets in front, don't run her down, jump off and put her on the sidewalk. Train your ears to hear the pistol in a man's pocket. Keep your foot on the brake and a curb on your temper; a timely joke can make it a dollar more. You'll get into tough places, so does a doctor. Your fare is your patient; save his life if you can. When it comes to a toss up, you know who gets the preference. Never argue with a crook; take whatever he gives. If it's nothing, say thank you and get away. Don't let pretty feet lead you astray. A man's strength depends on his disposition, and the time of night. If you fall for it, forget it. Do what you can't help, but—whatever you do, don't get found out. It's all contradiction; you do something now and you don't do it the next time. If the same thing happens twice, it's never the same thing. You've got to be not only a good chauffeur but a good actor, a good talker, a good curser, a good fighter, a good navigator, a good all-around regular feller, and then you don't half fill the bill. Now scoot."

"Yes sir," said Floyd, and plunged into the depths of the night city.

His first venture in the taxi business was a personal success.

"Taxi, sir, taxi, Miss, take you anywhere—where to, Miss?" The women jumped in at once; he picked up two, going to the theatre. Would he call for them at eleven-thirty?

"With great pleasure," answered Floyd. He helped them out, and stood with his hat in his hand. He forgot he was a chauffeur for a moment. Then he drove people uptown, downtown, all over town, guiding his car in and out of the great mass of congested traffic.

A young fellow rushed at him. "Drive for your life, my wife is dying."

It was up in the Bronx. Floyd put on the speed. He got away from two policemen and landed at a brick house with the blinds lowered. The man dashed up the steps.

"Is she alive? Thank God!"

He threw Floyd a bill.

"You did well, my man, keep the change."

Floyd felt like a public benefactor. Hacking was a noble profession.

He was hailed by two men who jumped in. He didn't like them. He heard the pistol; looked into the butt of it. They gave him a street number outside the city limits.

"Drive like Hell!" He did. The men jumped out into a vacant lot. "Now cut away, and don't squeal."

Floyd said "Thank you," and shot across the town. He was held up and questioned. No, he hadn't seen anybody. He had no compunctions. He wouldn't give the guys away; that wasn't sport. Then he took the car back to the garage, and went home in the subway. He had thirty dollars. He put fifteen in an envelope, addressed it to Tom, and wrote on a slip of paper:

Dear Tom: Here is half the boodle. It was a great experience. Ready to help out at any time.

Tom got back early to the garage, washed his khaki suit, hung it up to dry, cleaned his car, looked over the motor. He waited for Floyd, but he didn't show up; he was sure the car would come back damaged. He expected that, but he hoped Garrison wouldn't get hurt. Then he grew impatient. It didn't matter to 'that guy' how long he stayed out—*his* wife wasn't waiting for him. He said good night to the man in the garage, told him to look out for a 'green-hand,' and showed him where the bandages were. Then for a bit of exercise he walked up to the Bronx, taking a drink now and then to ease his mind. It was two o'clock when he opened the door of the little flat. The kitchen was spotless, the blue and white oilcloth shone like marble tiles. There was a tray on the table, with cold corned beef and three large baked potatoes; the coffee was gurgling on the gas stove. He devoured everything in sight, washed up the dishes, then went into the next room and stood at the bed. Maudy was in a deep sleep, how pretty she was. She must have been very tired or she would have heard him come in. She'd been scrubbing that damn kitchen floor again. She couldn't wait till Sunday morning; that was his job. He looked at her small hands. They were rough from the washing soda, and the nails were not manicured. He had to kiss them, he couldn't help it. She opened her eyes, smelt the hootch.

"Tom, you're going it; you'll break your neck one night, and I'll be a widow—take a bath." The sleepy eyes closed, she dropped off again.

Tom put a roll of bills under her pillow, slipped out of his clothes and fell on the sofa. He didn't take a bath, he'd gotten over that pastime; he had something better to do.

30

Floyd woke up the next morning, his head aching, his limbs weary. The experience had battered his body, but shook up his mind. His share of the "boodle" lay on the table—three five-dollar bills. He examined them curiously, turning them over and over—the first money he had ever earned. Was it money? No—he threw away much more than that paltry sum every day. But this was different; he had worked for it with the "sweat of his brow." He felt the pressure of the masses, who were earning their bread. This meant money to them. He remembered how the Colonel looked at him, when he told him to sell something—they were needing more and more. "You're destroying capital," said the Colonel. "You should preserve it, it's your only source of income."

Capital! capital! He wondered if they had blown in all his father had left—blown in, where?—into the air like soap bubbles, which glittered for a moment in the sun, then burst and disappeared.

He put his hand to his head. Where could he go to pass the morning? Julie was not visible until twelve. She was lucky; the day was only half as long for her. Then that queer feeling came again; he went to see Dr. McClaren.

"How's your wife?" said the doctor.

"Very well, as far as I can see. I want to speak to you about myself—my mind wanders—I cannot concentrate, nothing interests me; I go back always to the past; the things I have lived through haunt me."

"You are trying too hard to forget."

"I don't understand."

"No, you don't. If we wipe out memory, we throw into the dust heap of oblivion the best part of our life, experience."

"But if that experience is unbearable?"

"We can make it bearable. We must work it the right way."

"But I cannot see how! Father Cabello spoke about the 'gift of forgetting.'"

The doctor smiled. "I am not for such narcotics. We shouldn't go about hypnotizing ourselves. A man of mind should be able to deal with the complications of his nature in an intelligent manner."

This meant nothing to Floyd; the doctor was talking "over his head."

"I'll try to make it clearer to you. You have got yourself tangled up. What you think so terrible one day will be precious to you in years to come. How do you stand financially?"

"I don't know, I'm not sure—badly, I think."

The doctor knew; he had seen the Colonel.

"I want you to try to get rich."

Floyd had a shock. He looked sharply at the doctor; there was no glare in his eyes, but he was fingering a paper cutter—no, he wasn't mad—but he was a mind reader. Floyd had been thinking of money—in a vague way, wondering that so many people whose names he had never heard had bobbed up as millionaires.

"The pursuit of wealth may be sordid, but if we succeed, we are compensated by a gratifying sense of self-confidence, authority, power, not speaking of the good we can do with our 'ill gotten' gains. As for the spiritual side being starved, well, we don't think so; if we concentrate on the world of the spirit, it will demoralize us in our practical life, which is our end of it. We must uphold that, for the sake of bankrupt Europe."

"Doctor, I dreamt last night that I was enormously rich."

"Good! make it a complex. It will drive more harmful ideas out of your mind. Come and see me again. I am curious to know how my prescription's going to work...."

Floyd found the Colonel, erect, well satisfied; he had no complexes, he wasn't married.

"How do I stand?"

The Colonel hesitated.

"Come, out with it; I want the truth."

"Well, you'll have to practice strict economy to make up for your enormous expenditure of the last few years. Do you want to sell your house?"

"Economy? Sell the house? Julie!—impossible."

"Nowadays a man can't live on interest."

Floyd snapped his fingers.

"Economy, bah! We'll have to create new capital." The Colonel opened a drawer, took out a card of the Garrison estate, kept as a physician does the history of a patient's disease; then he placed a map on the table. It was interlaced with red lines designating the shrinkage. Floyd looked over it.

"The entire water-front is crossed off, I see."

"Yes, the Martin Steele Corporation bought it for investment. By the way, that was a great thing young Steele did."

"What thing?"

"He left his entire business to his employees, equal shares, and the money to keep it going. Waldbridge told me about it with tears in his eyes, the other day, at the memorial service they gave for him."

"Memorial service?"

"Didn't you know? I saw Mrs. Garrison there, but she was gone before I could get through the crowd."

Julie there? She hadn't told him. He thought he knew all her movements.

"It was wonderful; I wouldn't have missed it for the world. They are going to screen it. It was a queer mixed crowd—artists he had saved from starvation, musicians he had sent abroad, women he had started right—they all got up and told their stories. It was like a Christian Science service. A man sang, a barber named Hippolyte, well-known on Fifth Avenue, a wonderful voice. They say an opera manager has engaged him. He sang psalms in Greek and Hebrew, wails in the minor key, just tore at your entrails. He set them all crying. One poor cripple made a scene; swore he saw the dead man's spirit. Of course, that hypnotized the others; they all saw it. There was a tall man in a corner—the light struck him for a moment. I tell you, Garrison, I've got the hide of a rhinoceros, but it made my flesh creep. Now there are two left of those river shanties, we'll pull them down and build one big office building—"

Floyd didn't hear him; he was in the church listening to the voice of Hippolyte, the cries, the prayers for Martin—the philanthropist, the good man. He forced himself to say something.

"I knew Martin Steele all my life, but had no idea of that side of him."

"Nor I, but most men keep the best part of them hidden."

"Yes," said Floyd, tracing lines on the map. "I'll go down with you and look at those shanties. I want money and lots of it; every fool's got it. I can be as big a fool as the next one."

The Colonel didn't contradict him, but he doubted if Garrison would ever be that kind of a fool.

BOOK III

Future—the hidden meanings of Past and Present, a dark picture. Imagination flashes the light of Prophecy, foretells life's realization or disillusion, the Soul's victory or defeat.

"Fiction, my Masters! All is Fiction!"

BOOK III

1

IT took some years to become a "rich fool," but Garrison accomplished it. He had no business ability, at least that is what he told people, and honestly believed it; how could he? he had never been in business. He thought it well over, and became what he had always condemned in others—a gambler. He risked every dollar he had, and all he could borrow in hazardous real estate speculations. It was touch and go many times, as the values rose and fell. They called him "Lucky Garrison"; he knew better, but there was a grim satisfaction in his success. He realized as he had learnt to manipulate money that a man can attain nothing without it. Other "big" interests developed. Every bit of his energy came into play; there was always some interesting thing coming up, which led to great connections, such as international finance and the like. New "deals" got to be a necessary physical tonic, like a cocktail before dinner, and a strong cigar and black coffee after....

He scanned the morning paper at the breakfast table, looking carefully over the financial news and rate of exchange.

"We are sailing into prosperous times," said he to Julie. He was an optimist, like all good American millionaires. Julie had no opinion, she smiled.

As Dr. McClaren predicted, her religious mania passed off—she was now deeply interested in Art, a patroness of the Museum, and much sought after by budding talent. Floyd encouraged this "mania"; it was harmless. There was a busy day before him, a big deal to close; he was in a hurry to get to his office. She went with him to the door. He looked up at the imposing staircase and beautiful Tiffany glass window. He hated it once; how could he have been so prejudiced? It was all in the very best of taste, Julie was perfectly framed in it.

"I'll meet you at the Museum about five o'clock; we'll drive around for an hour. I forgot to tell you, I've invited some men to dinner; it's business. Do you mind?"

Julie smiled again.

"Oh, no!"

With a sudden impulse he took her hand.

"Are you happy, Julie?"

She looked at him; what made him ask that?

"Oh yes!—I have every reason to be."

"Is there anything I can buy for you?"

"Nothing."

She stood watching him drive off and waved her hand. It was well-known in their circle that the Garrisons were a very devoted couple.

Floyd leaned back in the car, puffing at a cigar. The years had changed him; the sensitive boy had become a man of affairs, a Capitalist. He was very sane; his Puritan instincts rebelled against the rioting emotions of the Latins. His life was made up of facts and figures; ultimately he would have become an image of clay, like his father's statues, but there was a secret element of his life, of which no one had the slightest clue. The Past had ceased to torture him; it became a consolation. He lived over and over again the Romance of his youth, the agony, the passion, his first years with Julie, the rage of the murderer, the whole tragedy, but it didn't hurt him now; Martin was dead, forgiven. We count the years we have lived to know how old we are—correct mathematics, but our age corresponds to other numbers. Heart swings are the rhythm of our seasons, recording in spiritual time, the real life.

The car stopped in Twelfth Street. Floyd jumped out, stood for a moment looking up at the imposing twenty-story office building which he had erected on the site of his old home. It had rented well. There was not a room empty. He had retained an office for himself on the third floor. He sat down to his desk, read his mail. He was about to sell the building—the psychological moment had come to "turn it over" and get a handsome profit. He never kept any real estate very long. New York neighborhoods change and values fluctuate. Then it occurred to him quite suddenly that the room in which he sat was about the height of his father's workshop in the little house where he was born. There was no emotion, but it was strange he had never thought of it before. He looked at the heavy safe, the walls lined with repositories, where contracts were kept—and saw—clay images. He looked down at his desk; it was littered with old rags, bits of arms, legs—a young man, with an agonized face, dropped a candle.

He smiled. What courage youth has! It was well done. The home of his childhood was still his; he had not desecrated it. He saw Mary flying past him up the stairs; she had become a world figure, the head of an international organization of nurses. When Julie's "headaches" came on, Mary was always there. He'd go softly to the door and wait; he didn't knock; he knew she'd come out.

"Mrs. Garrison is much better; I'm sure she'll be all right in the morning." Then the worn face, dim eyes, streaked hair would vanish. She stood again at the window in her bare room, where they had loved each other for a moment.

The telephone at his elbow startled him. Julie's voice—would he order some flowers for the dinner table.

"Certainly, and a bunch for you. Anything else?"

"Yes," her tone became confidential. "What wine do you want served?—are the gentlemen heavy drinkers?"

"No, but they'll take all you give them."

He dropped the receiver, smiling. How eager he used to be to do all those small errands! the night of their house-warming—he drank too much. That Swede was a nice man. The den on the top floor was hung now with maps of suburban towns, new fields for speculation; he spent many evenings poring over them. Somehow his business mind always worked well up there in that room where a man was murdered by his wife.

The stenographer put a paper before him. He started, came back to reality; it was a bill of sale and very satisfactory.

"I'll close the deal tonight."

Then he commenced searching in an old desk for some papers he wanted, and came across a sealed envelope; on it was written "Boodle."

Boodle? What did it mean? He broke the seal and took out three five-dollar bills.

Tom Dillon! He had quite forgotten him, but he had a vague idea that he owned a Taxi Company, and was strong in local politics.

He put back the fifteen dollars, resealed the envelope, and wrote on it, "The foundation of the Garrison fortune." He would give the story to his publicity man—how an impoverished son of wealth started in life by earning fifteen dollars as a chauffeur. Tom Dillon! was the real thing. What *was* the real thing? Had *he* found it? or was he chasing phantoms? He had that feeling sometimes, in his most successful moments; it was a queer sensation, as if he had caught a thing of vapor that melted out of hand and challenged him again from far off—and again that shadow race!

He thought often of Tom Dillon after that, and one election night he saw him in the crowd, with a fine young fellow, the image of his father; they were laughing and nudging each other like two boy friends. Floyd shook off a feeling of loneliness and got out of their way.

2

Julie was recovering from an attack which left her mentally exhausted. She lay back in the sedan, her deep-rimmed eyes like smouldering coals. She arrived at the Museum an hour before the time agreed on with Floyd, wandered through the rooms, making notes about the hanging and grouping of new pictures. There was a small canvas in a corner which she thought was somewhat crowded in. She asked about it. It had been received very recently and was not yet catalogued. "Yes, it was badly hung."

She sank down on a divan before the picture—a Swiss landscape, with a mountain background sloping down to a grassy plateau; below, a bank of mist, through which could be distinguished an old chapel, with a broken cross on top. In a corner, hardly visible to the naked eye, she read, "Val Sinestra," and underneath, two letters, M. S.

She bent nearer, looking eagerly into the picture. Was it her imagination! or did she really see a shadowy outline of a man with a white figure in his arms? Martin! Martin! with flaming eyes, distorted face!—desperate! mad!

"A charming picture, isn't it? like a Corot. It's the first of this artist, he's not known in America."

It was a member of the committee who spoke. Then Floyd came up and introduced his business friends. She smiled, asked them if they had seen some gems in the next room, and led them away from that picture in the corner.

On arriving home she went through the house looking for something and finally found it, hidden away on a top shelf covered with dust; it was a small glass vase with a delicate stem. The engraving was beautiful like a white mist over it. The butler washed it and held it up to the light; colors flashed through it.

"It's Bohemian glass, Madame. It will break easily."

"No! It's very strong, I've had it a long time."

She put it on her bed-table, with a dark red rose in it. From that time the "headaches" were less frequent, the ravings about punishment ceased. Mary said to the doctor:

"I think she's getting over those horrible nightmares."

"I'm glad of that," said the doctor wearily. He himself was suffering from an attack of nerves. He was getting old, and the hives of human bees he cared for didn't always contain honey. They stung him at his patients' table, at births, at marriages; at deaths, less so—that was a release. He fought them with his Scotch tenacity, but they grew too much for him. Finally he got rid of them by retiring from active practice and putting the whole "bunch" without names or dates, into a book on psychical research, which became celebrated.

Julie devoted much time to her boy—took him in her car every morning to St. John's College, called for him in the afternoon, preached religion to him at home, warned him of the great evils which arise from lack of it. She had been very negligent in her youth, and was punished for it. Religion was a great consolation.

He listened to her with deference. He was extraordinarily gifted and devoured everything he could lay his hands on in the way of serious reading. His father was proud of him, but there was a growing sense of uneasiness about his religious studies. He saw little of the boy, who spent his evenings in his own room, filled with books he had bought himself in the old book shops. Floyd couldn't understand them. The maps which hung on the walls of his den were more intelligible.

A distant cousin of Julie's came to America ostensibly on business. The Bank, taken over by the family, had grown enormously rich under American management. Mr. Gonzola was highly cultured—a dark, handsome man with white hands and long tapering fingers. He was delighted with the boy and his knowledge of international literature. He found him reading Renan.

"That's forbidden, isn't it?"

The boy answered with a gleam of humor.

"Not forbidden, but not taught. I read all they recommend in school, and all they forget, out of it."

Then came a letter from Father Cabello to Julie. He was very glad to hear that everything continued to be so satisfactory with her. The wonderful gifts of her boy interested him; he saw in his genius the hand of God leading him into the Divine path. They must decide now about his career.

Julie handed the letter to Floyd, who read it carefully and understood its hidden significance.

"This means the priesthood."

"Yes," said Julie, "but don't speak of that to Joseph."

That evening at dinner, she said:

"Joseph, would you like to go to Rome to visit Father Cabello?"

The boy's eyes lit up.

"Oh yes, it's the dream of my life. And—I would like to go to Vienna, to see your people."

Mr. Gonzola spoke quietly, his arm around the boy.

"Let me take him, Julie. I promise you there will be no influence. Our family has been split into different religious camps for generations; those who have remained true to their faith have made no effort to bring the others back. We do not proselytize. The missionary is unknown to us."

Julie hesitated, looked at Floyd; it was a great responsibility. The boy was bending over eagerly watching his father, who decided quickly, as was his way in business. His theory was, when a man weighs the pros and cons of an enterprise, the difficulties grow so great that he generally ends in not undertaking it. He would give the boy his chance; he was old enough now to decide for himself.

"Go with Mr. Gonzola," said Floyd.

The boy flung his arms around his father; "I will do what is right!"

"I'm sure you will, my boy," answered Floyd. At that moment he caught sight of Julie's face reflected in the mirror; it was lit by a quick flash of joy.

3

When Father Cabello received a letter from Julie informing him Joseph had sailed with a Gonzola, he proceeded at once to counteract any possible "baleful" influence. He communicated with the Catholic members of the family in Vienna, hinting that the boy was destined for the church. This branch of the Gonzolas were devout Catholics, generations old; they welcomed Joseph affectionately and brought him as early as possible to Rome. There he remained for some time, a member of Father Cabello's household, coming and going at will. The priest watched, waited; the mind of the boy was not yet ripe for decision.

Joseph was dazzled with his first glimpse of the Pagan City—its remains of Hellenic civilization; the pomp and splendor of its churches; the Cardinals in their decaying palaces, clinging to the traditions of the Past; the art of the great Masters, those faithful servants of the Church, with their wonderful portrayal of legendary religion. The unearthly beauty of their divine types, fired the boy's imagination, stimulated him like rich wine, tasted for the first time, taken again in long draughts until his senses reeled. The people fascinated him with their magnetism, their emotional sensuality, their worship of women, symbolized in the Blessed Virgin and Child; their passions—jealousy, hate, revenge, repentance. He roamed day after day through the streets, sat for hours in the churches listening to the chanting of the priests, with a pleasant sense of drowsiness, like the after effects of a narcotic. He followed the processions of monks, pilgrims, peasants, into churches, away from churches, sprinkling with holy water, kissing burnt pieces of sacred wood—and always that music! Oh! that music! swelling in waves of overpowering sadness from the throats of unsexed men—the terrible sweetness of it, sucking him down into the waters of oblivion, of self-deception; the soul in safety, interceded for, the load of personal responsibility fallen away, care-free on earth, secure of Heaven, an unutterable sense of rest from that torturing brain which keeps persecuting with its unceasing cry, "Think while 'tis day, for the night cometh when no man can think."

In moments of realization, he would say to the priest, "Father, I am going to Vienna; I must go." The priest did not keep him back. The boy must live through the inevitable experience of intoxication, reaction, submission. He was travelling smoothly; he would arrive safely.

4

When Joseph went from Rome to Vienna to visit the Gonzolas, he was in a state of mental unrest and indecision. The artist in him shrank from activity. He was very sensitive; he couldn't bear pain, disappointment. The Church would be a shelter from the materialism of the world. It would be ideal to work for the poor. The garb of piety appealed to his imagination—a priest walking among the wretched, the persecuted, the unhappy, giving everything, his material wealth, himself, living a simple contemplative life. The beauty of it all still remained with him, keeping him in a semi-intoxicated emotional state. He thought of the works of immortal art created in the quiet of the cloister. He was sorely tempted, not by the flesh like St. Anthony, but by the spirit and the longing for release from a leaden sense of responsibility.

"If not that, what?" He saw nothing for him in the future. His father had at least the satisfaction of success. He himself had created his capital. It was a game, like racing, roulette, politics—a game, life a game! what else? what else?—It was all so ugly; the yearning for beauty came again, he was sorely tempted....

Mr. Gonzola's wife and three daughters were models of domesticated womanhood. Their home was very modern, with just enough of the idealism of religion to give it spiritual charm. The girls were well educated, practical women, keenly alive to the responsibility of their wealth, full of enthusiasm and hope for the future of the world. They received Joseph with great cordiality, helped him perfect his German, and were silently sympathetic toward his unsettled spiritual condition of mind.

Mrs. Gonzola was one hundred per cent maternal: she mothered her husband, her daughters, her friends, her poor, and any stray animal who instinctively came to her for shelter. Joseph was her life's crowning joy, the realization of a hope long dead—a son! She found him too thin, too pale; poor boy, he had never known the cuisine of Israel, the finest in the world. No Cordon-bleu can equal the Jewish mother, who cooks with the subtlety and cleanliness of religious tradition and puts into her cakes the honey of love. This healthy sane atmosphere was a good tonic for Joseph's over-excited mind.

Mr. Gonzola's ethics were very simple. He kept the two principles of life wide apart, and gave "to God what was His, to men, what was theirs." He was an able man of business, and did not consider a good bargain with legitimate profit, ungodly. Sometimes he had an uneasy feeling; the religious ground was slipping like sand from under his feet. He said to Joseph with a sigh:

"I do not live up to ritual laws as strictly as I should. My daughters won't let me; but I am going to take you to Frankfort to visit the head of the family, Pedro Gonzala, who has preserved the original spelling of our name and the tradition of our ancestors. In his home you will see pure orthodoxy, but— don't forget the responsibility is on my shoulders. I have given my word to your mother—and I want to keep it—if possible."

Joseph laughed. Mr. Gonzola was an honest man.

5

The family of bankers, with branches all over the world, were assembled this year in Frankfort. Pedro Gonzala, despite his great age, was consulted about every detail by the "young" men of the firm, from fifty years old and upward. The "children" under fifty stood meekly silent, and listened to warnings against the ardor of youth and the temptation of speculative times. The house of Gonzola had braved many storms, was sometimes drawn into international financial catastrophes, but it had always kept its honor unimpeached and continued to live up to its reputation as creditors of the world. These cold men of finance led a dual existence. When they stepped over the thresholds of their palatial homes, the world outside was forgotten.

They lived their religious life with extreme exactness. Their wives and daughters were faithful to the Law, in their domestic life, their marriage life, and in the education of their children. They were the remains of a vanishing caste, which lived upon its own fanaticism.

When Joseph first met Pedro Gonzala in his private office, he saw a very old man wearing a black silk skull cap, otherwise well groomed and modern in appearance. He was seated at his desk, surrounded by the members of the firm who listened to him with great respect.

The "old gentleman" came to business every day in his carriage, although he had many cars but was never known to ride in them. He was interested in the breeding of horses, frequented the races, and patronized art, music, and the theatre. Most of his time was devoted to philanthropic enterprises, but he kept a firm hand on the ship of finance, of which he remained until the end of his life the undisputed head.

He questioned Joseph about his mother, remarking upon the success of the Gonzola bank in New York. He knew all about "lucky Garrison" who had shown himself very able. He invited Joseph to dinner at his home.

The Gonzala mansion was sheltered from the gaze of the curious, by a closely planted row of very old trees, whose entwined branches symbolized the unity of the family, a treasure-house of antiques, from all parts of the world— collected with taste and discernment by each succeeding generation. The picture gallery was celebrated for its rare masterpieces. Joseph took great delight in a corner of family portraits. But the most cherished treasure of Pedro Gonzala's home was Ruth, his granddaughter, just approaching womanhood; she was all that was left of his immediate family. The World War had swept the younger men away. He had lived ten years longer than the allotted Biblical time; he was life-worn, but before he went to his long rest, his little Ruth must be married to a righteous man, a student of the Talmud, and—of *equal birth*. Such a one was difficult to find.

Pedro Gonzala stood in the grand salon surrounded by beautiful dark-eyed women and serious men of finance. He welcomed Joseph in the name of the family, as a great grandson of that learned man and deep thinker, Joseph Abravanel, who fought with all his strength against the wave of assimilation which had engulfed his immediate family.

"You, my boy, are in the third generation of those who were led away from the old tradition; it is not your fault, but no student or thinker can afford to neglect the study of a race which gave to the world the first revelation of one God. Hebrew thought, in its inception, its ethics, its morals, is the pure wine of religion; in America, they have thinned it with the water of reform, and put it into fine-looking bottles with gold labels."

There was a ripple of applause; the old gentleman told his little jokes like an actor, expecting response, which the family gave at the proper time; then he related the oft-repeated story of his youth, when his dear Sarah, "God rest her soul," was alive. He led the boy before a portrait painted by Rembrandt, representing a stately, handsome matron. At a ball in Paris, given to them by the diplomats and aristocrats of France, there were rumors of war, and much disquietude. He himself was absent, called away to a serious Cabinet consultation. The guests crowded about Mrs. Gonzala, who was gracious and smiling.

"Are you not worried, Madame?" asked a celebrated diplomat.

"Oh! No," laughed Mrs. Gonzala. "I am certain there will be no war, because I will not permit my husband to lend the money for it."

Ruth stepped daintily down the marble staircase. Her grandfather had bade her array herself. It was a gala occasion—the reunion of the family, and a welcome to a young Gonzola from America. Around her neck were rows of costly pearls; diamonds sparkled in her hair; she wore a cape of ermine, a young queen of an old dynasty—an inheritance of beauty and purity. She put out her hand to Joseph, and said "Welcome, cousin Joseph"—raising her face to his. He bent down and kissed her cheek; they stood looking at each other, speechless. The women nudged each other. "What an ideal couple they might have been"—it was a great pity.

The long dinner table was a beautiful picture with its service of gold, priceless glass and fine linen, and the Patriarchal figure at its head. Ruth sat beside him.

"I am dazzled," said Joseph, "such lovely women, such jewels, such wealth."

"We are not wealthy," answered Ruth, "because it is a principle of the family to give away a large part of its income, and you will see that we live very simply; but tonight all this is in your honor. Our jewels, furs, laces have come down to us from generations back; our home and pictures can never be sold, unless the business goes under, and that will never happen."

"I hope not," said Joseph, "it has meant too much to the world; but all these jewels must have been bought once."

"Oh, yes, in the times of the Ghetto, when the Jews were not allowed to own real estate—so they bought jewels and hung them around the necks of their wives who wore them in secret and gave them to their daughters and daughters' daughters. This has an interesting history." She touched a necklace of shining, pink, living things lying against her white skin. "When the Romans separated Queen Berenice from her kingly lover, the last thing he did was to throw these pearls around her neck. She went back to her own dominion and the pearls after her death became the property of the Temple. We have had them in our family for many generations."

He bent down to examine the pearls, but his gaze stopped at her soft dark eyes.

"And you will give them to your daughter?"

"Yes," said Ruth, "but I don't think I shall ever marry."

"Why—" insisted Joseph.

"Because," her voice dropped, he bent lower to listen, "I can only marry one of my own faith; they are all dying out. They have forgotten their ancestry."

6

Father Cabello had reached the zenith of his earthly ambition, the Cardinalate. He had easily won in the race for advancement—a man of wealth and winning personality. The magic word "America" gave him prestige; it was a sign of goodwill to the church in the United States. The priest was generally beloved, his doors were always open to the poor, to whom he gave liberal hands; they crowded the steps of his house, penetrated into his apartments. All efforts of his attendants to keep them away was futile.

"Let them in," said the Father, "they will be my future associates, 'for of such is the Kingdom of Heaven.'"

His secretary, a member of an old patrician family, shrugged his shoulders; his unspoken thought was, "if I have to live with them in Heaven, I hope I'll never die."

The Cardinal had been confined to his room for some days with an attack of weakness, the result of an overtaxed heart. The doctor said to him, "Your Eminence, you must shun all excitement—no more receptions, no more arduous night work, no activity of any kind."

The Cardinal smiled, "That would be premature death; I must take my chances. But at present I cannot work; I have no strength."

His new honors had not changed his mode of living. His *palazzo*, a relic of past grandeur, was simply furnished with only the necessary chairs and tables, and completely bare of drapery or superfluous decorations. The Roman sun flooded his rooms through the high-arched windows. The garden of boxwood hedges and old trees was beautiful and fragrant; he could stand on his terrace and see the cupolas and innumerable spires of the city of churches, and listen to the bells pealing—now soft, caressing, pleading—now loud, harsh, commanding—those eternal bells that have welcomed into the world, and followed out of it, millions of souls.

The Cardinal sat in his private apartment. His fingers tapped nervously on the polished wood of the table upon which was a dish of fruits—figs, honey, and a silver jug of iced water—a habit he had brought from the land of his adoption. He was waiting for Joseph. In the excitement of his new honors, weeks had passed with only now and then the accustomed epistolary greetings, but the time was approaching to speak of the future. If he could realize his plan, thought out in every detail, this boy would inherit his wealth, would carry on his work among the poor.

A spasm of agony turned his lips blue, his face livid. He quickly dropped a tablet into a glass of water and swallowed it. The unbearable pain slowly subsided; the brain moved again.

"If God would be merciful and let him live to see the boy ordained."

A flash of determination, of invincible Will. Yes, it would be! It must be! He forgot the dark-cornered room; he saw the cathedral, the procession of priests, the young divine. Why didn't the boy come? He was eager to stamp his plan with the seal of realization. A shaft of sunlight shooting through the window struck the chair opposite him. His sick heart bounded. Seated there he saw his old friend and enemy, Joseph Abravanel. He slowly made his way to the chair, passing his hand over it; it was empty. His thought had conjured up a momentary vision. How often had they sat like that, opposite each other at a table set with fruit and wine, the long evening passing like a flash over the chess board which became symbolical of the spiritual struggle between them. The tenacity of that old man, who would not give up hope, even after the conversion of his daughter!

"You have won this time, but there is the next generation."

When Julie was born, he was cheated again in this game for souls; but he would not give in, "God's chosen people cannot die; they may lose the path, but they will find it again; they will come back in the third generation."

A spasm of fear convulsed the priest. Joseph Abravanel had the prophetic clairvoyance of his race. No! No! The boy was a good, faithful child of the Church, a believer in the true Faith.

He glanced again at the chair opposite; again he met those eyes long extinct—spirit eyes.

The servant announced, "Joseph Abravanel Gonzola Garrison."...

Joseph threw himself with a gush of irresistible love into the old man's arms; then, remembering, he dropped on his knees and kissed the ring of His

Eminence. The Cardinal raised him, looking long into that mobile face aglow with the joy of life.

"Sit down, Joseph, we have much to talk over. No! no! not there, here."

He pointed to a chair close beside him; there were three now at the table—indomitable spirits; one, invisible.

The Cardinal felt his way, asked about the family; he had not heard from Julie for some time.

"Oh, Mother is a bad correspondent, but if I miss a mail she cables." His laughter rang through the high-vaulted room. "Father wants me to go into the banking business; the Gonzolas think I have talent for it."

He was peeling an apple, careful not to break the ring; the Cardinal noticed his long tapering fingers, his white hands.

"Well, what do you think about it?"

The boy's eyes shot a mischievous gleam.

"Our great ancestor on my father's side was a baker, on my mother's side they added a letter to it, and it became banker. Now if it is true that the third generation goes back, I think I'd rather make cakes than money."

The Cardinal laughed; the boy's merriment was contagious. Then he grew grave again.

"My son, there is something in each generation which belongs neither to the Past nor the Present, but to the Future; it is God's will working in us. The time has come to tell you of my wishes for you. I want you to continue my work, to take up the staff of Divine Duty, to lay upon the altar of renunciation the great gifts bestowed upon you by an All-Seeing God; you will give your youth, your manhood, your old age, to save those helpless souls who need your intercession, your spiritual support. You will one day succeed me in Rome; it has been my only earthly dream, ever since I held you as an infant in my arms. My time is short; I want to see you enter upon the path before I die."

The boy was on his feet, his face quivering with grief, the tears streaming from his eyes.

"No, no; you must not die! I love you! I love you! If I could prolong your life for one hour I would give my right hand."

He held it up, firm, strong, beautiful. The Cardinal's imagination played him a trick again. He saw another white hand held up, old, feeble, trembling; the light shone through it.

The boy's heart was heavy—that beloved face before him, with the pallor of death on it. How could he say what he must?...

"I have thought long and deeply of your wishes for me. I cannot! I cannot! There is something in me that rebels against the chastisement of the flesh. I don't want to think always of death, to pray always; I want to work, I want to live. No one can intercede for me; I can intercede for no one. Each must work out his own salvation. The old world is spiritually decaying; the young must be the pioneers of a new world. We must tear down and dig and set the stones of a new foundation, and those who come after us will build. The Future will see miracles; the human being will awaken to the truth, that he himself is God."

"Stop! Blasphemer!" The old man broke into choking sobs. "Joseph! Joseph! I am responsible for your soul's salvation; this is all madness! You will repent when it is too late."

"Father! it hurts me to give you pain, but it is impossible. I cannot! I cannot!"

The Cardinal was cold to the soul—his boy, his heart's idol, a heretic, an infidel; the stripling was strange to him, standing there with a look in his face of iron determination. He would break that will; he must!

"You do not know what you are doing. You are too young. You have been influenced by that old sophisticated fox, Pedro Gonzala. I fought a greater man than he and won; I will fight again—I will save you, as I saved your mother."

"No! No! They have not influenced me. I have given up dogma, I will not be chained again by ritual, I will not be a mummy wrapped in the superstition of past ages. I am a living, thinking being. I am free! free!"

The priest's eyes went past him to that shadowy figure, looking down now, as it had so often done in life, at a chess board on the table, fingering the pieces, moving, removing, trying new combinations. Neither had won; it was a drawn game;—stalemate. With a low moan he sank back in his chair.

The boy gave a cry of terror.

"Father, speak to me! Speak to me!"

The priest heard him not. He had renounced this world for the glory of the next. He was going to his reward, where there would be no dogma, no ritual, no religion.

A terrible fear clutched the boy. He looked about despairingly. He was forsaking the shelter of those old walls. He had stripped himself bare. He must go out naked to meet the stones of the Philistines. He threw himself down before the beloved guide of his childhood, sobbing out his love, his loneliness.

"Come back! Come back! Don't leave me! I am afraid, afraid!"

He called in vain; those wonderful dreams—the hope of immortality, the joy of Heaven—would never come back; they had gone into the past, like that still form, deaf to his entreaties, to his cries—gone forever!

7

Mr. Garrison was getting into his coat in the hall; it was after nine.

"Good-bye, Julie, I'm off."

Her answer came from above.

"Don't go yet. I want to speak to you; it is something important."

With a suppressed feeling of impatience, he took off his coat and went up the stairs. He wondered how much Julie would ask for. She was very extravagant. He was surprised to find her waiting at the door of the sitting-room for him. She had slipped out of bed and thrown on a filmy wrapper; he was struck anew by her youthfulness. Her skin was like satin. She was forty and could easily be taken for ten years younger; but her beauty had ceased to disturb him. It was an accepted fact, like his luck in business.

As he bent to kiss her, she noticed his hair was getting thin on the top. He would soon be bald.

He dropped down on the sofa beside her.

"You looked tired this morning; didn't you sleep well?" said Julie.

"As well as usual."

Floyd's mind was overstrained; his accumulating interests kept him on a severe tension. His eyes troubled him and he wore strong owl-like spectacles framed in tortoise shell which gave him a look of comic solemnity. He didn't tell Julie how very badly he slept; his many speculations took gibbering forms and danced around his pillow. He spent whole nights in his den, where a man had "sweated blood." He was beginning to feel the significance of that expression. At first the thought of possessing a million made his head reel, now he laughed at his modest pretensions. Desire grows until it ceases to be servant and becomes master. He hunted gain like a gambler who risks his last dollar. Envious competitors said, "Garrison's getting to be a skin-flint; he'd sell his soul for money."

It came back to him from a friend; he wasn't annoyed, but wondered in a vague way if it were really true.

When the news arrived of Cardinal Cabello's sudden death and Joseph's decision, Julie took it very hard; she spent days in the convent praying for her son's soul.

Floyd consulted with Dr. McClaren.

"She'll get over it. It's only a temporary disturbance. A bit of good news now will set her all right again. And how are you, Mr. Garrison? My medicine worked well, I see."

"Oh! yes," said Floyd, "but times are bad—a man must be careful how he invests his money."

"That never troubles me; I haven't any to invest."

"You've been a successful doctor, haven't you?"

"I hope so."

The trouble with Dr. McClaren was that his bills were ridiculously small.

"He underestimates his own ability," said Floyd to Julie. "A man must set the price of his life's work, and as he appraises himself, the world values him."

"I have a letter from Joseph," answered Julie.

"So have I; he keeps me well posted on complications abroad; I am sure, if he will only get down to it, he'll make a first-class financier."

This was Floyd's ambition for his son.

She took a letter from the table beside her. It was long, covering many sheets of paper.

"The Gonzalas have been very good to him; he is in much better spirits. It was terrible, that struggle with His Eminence. I would have given in."

She always thought now of Cabello as "His Eminence," in glittering robes, sparkling with jewels.

"Yes," said Floyd. "You always gave in. That was the trouble." He turned to go.

"Stop a moment; you must hear this."

He pushed away the call of business; he would rather have read it himself, when he found time, at luncheon perhaps. He hated to be read to. He couldn't concentrate; his mind wandered off in figures. She read in a low voice very rapidly, stopping now and again; he knew she was skipping something; he wasn't offended. He had always felt like a third party, and thought of Joseph as "Julie's boy." It was an interesting letter written in picturesque metaphors, just the way Julie's mother used to speak, thought Floyd. The boy told of his many visits to Frankfort, and of closer acquaintance with Pedro Gonzala, and his granddaughter. They had given a costume ball to celebrate her sixteenth birthday.

"A costume ball—that's rather sporty," remarked Floyd. He had in mind those French masquerades given in his youth, where Martin danced the Can-Can with indecent French women.

"Oh, no," answered Julie, "listen; Joseph explains it.

"This was a ball, where the family personated their ancestors, the portraits in the gallery. Ruth took me around, told me their history for generations back. Wonderful, so full of struggle, tragedy, romance. I couldn't hear enough of it!"

"It didn't affect me like that—those portraits you sent away gave me a cold chill."

"They were not your ancestors," said Julie with a touch of sarcasm. Then she went on reading.

"They called one of the portraits 'the unhappy Pedro Gonzala,' because he was an illegitimate son. That was Grandfather! I couldn't tear myself away from him; he had such brave defiant eyes. Dearest Mother, I think it is a great injustice to brand a human being like that. There is nothing illegitimate in Nature. I'd rather be the child of love, than of calculation born in wedlock."

Floyd frowned.

"I don't approve of those views. I'm afraid the boy is catching European radicalism."

Julie didn't answer; she was absorbed in the letter. Floyd looked at his watch and jumped up.

"Wait, wait, it is not finished.

"Mother, I've written you often about Ruth, but I'm sure you don't know what she is like. When I am with her, I'm afraid to look at her, and when I'm away, I can't imagine how she looks. She's something indescribable. Mother, I have fought with all my might against her, because I knew it was hopeless, but when she said she loved me, I went straight to her grandfather. I told him about the struggle with my conscience and our dear friend's sudden death—he was very much moved, and put his hand over my head and blessed me; then I took courage and asked him for Ruth. He was silent a long time before he answered. I could see he was thinking deeply. Then he said: 'The uncompromising adherence of our people to the Law in the days of the Ghetto preserved the virility of the Race; but today our blood is in the veins of the world. That obstinate orthodoxy with which we are reproached has saved us from being swept away in a great tidal wave of assimilation. Come to us! We will leave you free in all worldly matters, but you must live according to our ritual, you must worship in our synagogue, you must bring up your children in our tradition. You will realize as you get older the righteousness of my demands.'"

Floyd was annoyed.

"They *will* keep harping on those future generations. How can we lay down the law for our grandchildren; they'll know a lot more than we do."

Julie evidently didn't agree, she kept on reading.

"I walked about for days—trying to find some way—I wanted Ruth! Mother—you don't know how much! I couldn't keep away from her—she was waiting for me in the garden; she knew I would come. Mother, there was something so pure about her; such sweetness, I have never seen in any human thing. She was pale, but she spoke quietly. 'Joseph, I know what Grandfather has asked you to do for my sake; you mustn't do it. It wouldn't be right for you. We try to bring the Past into the Present, to preserve our religion. We think we live, but it is only a waking dream, and we are happy they let us dream; but dreams are not for you. Joseph, you must go out on the high road of Progress—and I—I must stay here with my grandfather.' Then I fell into the depths of despair and cried, how I cried. 'I won't let you; it is a living death; you are young! young!' Mother, I'll never forget her face when she answered. 'I look young, but my soul is old.'"

A sob choked Julie's voice; herself at sixteen, with that "old soul."

Floyd took the letter and read it rapidly to the finish.

"She has shown me the way; it is all clear to me now, and I am not unhappy. We are only separated for a little while; and Mother, I want you to write a letter to her grandfather—and plead for us. It might do some good. You are always asking me what I want. I want Ruth; give me Ruth!"

It was pathetic how the boy clung to his childish illusions. His mother could give him everything. Julie was crying silently.

The letter dropped from Floyd's hand; waves of memory swept over him. The struggle between Joseph Abravanel and Father Cabello against him— the bitterness, the tragedy. He was on his feet; there was a youthful ring in his voice which had long been absent. He flung his spectacles, that badge of age, on the table. His eyes were young again.

"We must bring it about; the boy must not be disappointed. He must have his love dream; he must not lose the best part of his life."

With a cry of joy Julie came to him and put her arms around his neck; they stood together, the light of that young romance across the sea reflected in their faces. Floyd bent down and whispered: "I was an ardent lover, wasn't I, Julie? You were so sweet, so sweet."

Then he remembered a business deal, and put on his spectacles. At the door he stopped.

"I shall write at once to Pedro Gonzala and make him a business proposition, which it would be madness to refuse; it will be a brilliant future for Joseph. This will cure him. He will see now that money can buy him everything! Don't cry, Julie; it's all for the best, and don't miss the mail. It's a five-cent stamp to Germany."

The Colonel lunched that day at the club, with Floyd, who was full of his plan to "dazzle" the Gonzolas. The Colonel was very sympathetic, then he said with a touch of sadness,

"I'm getting old. People have no use for a bachelor, when he ceases to be eligible. If I had a boy like yours, a wife like yours, I'd be a happy man."

Floyd thought a moment.

"I have been lucky; I come out well from very serious complications."

The Colonel thought he meant business deals.

"You often risked too much; you were once on the brink of disaster."

"More than once," answered Floyd, "but now things seem to be going my way. I would like to do some philanthropic construction work; a man must have something to keep him from drying up."

There was a responsive flash from the Colonel.

"I thought I was the only one who thought like that."

Floyd looked around at the crowded room; there was laughter, jingling of glasses, the perfume of good tobacco.

"I think they all do!"

8

Joseph had spent the winter in Geneva, studying the classic and modern languages. In the spring he joined a band of students, on a walking tour through the mountains. At Tarasp he bade them good-bye—he was going to see the Val Sinestra, where his mother, years before, had been caught in a storm and where his father's best friend, his Uncle Martin, had been lost in the mountains.

He passed the hotel, climbed down into the ravine, and stood before the little chapel, where by a strange coincidence they had met Father Cabello. He pushed open the door. How old it was, how very old!—the fading wall pictures, the broken windows, the time-stained Virgin and Child looming up out of the shadows. There was a sudden impulse to go to her, to speak to her, as he used to, when she was living to him. He gazed and gazed; she was drawing him down the aisle—

He went out, shutting the door softly behind him. Ghosts followed him as he climbed up the open road; then they melted away in the warm sunlight.

He was soon going home. His father's "dazzling" business proposition had been enthusiastically received by the younger Gonzolas—but the "old gentleman" remained obdurate. The boy must accept his conditions. Floyd had written to Joseph, advising him to "give in while the old man lived." But Joseph refused to make any concession; Ruth wouldn't let him.

He strolled along, his knapsack on his back, his hat and cape in his belt, a handsome young student; one meets them often in the mountains—fine happy lads, their only wealth, the Future. He knelt down by a stream, caught the falling water in his hands, and drank it; then he poetized.

Spring dances in the mountains.

Winter's young daughter, peeps at her

Sweet face in the Lake mirror.

The old Snow-man growls;

His blanket is thin, his feet stick out;

They are warm, he is melting.

He flies to the heights, in his

March-wind aeroplane.

There he can keep cool.

The bride robes herself in

Green and gold.

Flowers fall from her long curls.

The nuptial couch is white

With blossoms.

Wedding bells, birds caroling—

Cattle calls—Alpine horns,

Love time!

He threw back his head and laughed—Ruth would like it. He would bring her and show her where he wrote it—on their wedding day!

He read it again; it was a whimsical thing. He was sorry for the poets of the past who were chained in rhyme. The world had been rhyming so long, about everything—love, religion, the soul, the origin of man. People rhymed themselves into a state of poetic fiction; then suddenly they found out it was all rhyme and no reason.

9

The path ran along the side of the mountain. In the valley below he saw people running, heard the sound of music in the distance. He stopped a barefoot boy, who told him it was fête day in the Canton, to welcome their great Switzer home from Geneva, the artist Staehli.

"Staehli? Yes, I know. I admired his paintings at the exhibition."

Then he saw a procession of peasants in gala array, cows adorned with flowers, maidens singing, dancing. A tall man walked amongst them with swinging step, a peasant like the others. He puts his hand to his mouth and gives out a long piercing yodel. Above at a châlet a woman answers.

"That is Angela, his wife; she is the doctor of the Dorf; she heals with her hands and brews herb tea which has a magic power!"

"Oh! I'd like to meet the artist. Do you think he'll receive me?"

"Oh, yes! All are welcome; they have the best milk and cheese in the village. I'll take you down."

Near the châlet, they were stopped by an enormous hay wagon drawn by oxen. The young peasant leading them moved aside, smiling at Joseph.

"That's Martin Staehli, born and raised here," said the boy.

The artist was standing outside the châlet watching the procession wind its way around the path and out of sight.

"Could I rest here awhile? I've walked from Tarasp."

"I shall have great pleasure." He spoke English hesitatingly with a Swiss accent.

They entered a very large room, the light streaming in from all sides.

"This is my studio. My home is a little distance away in our family châlet. It is old; I will show it to you if you are interested in antiques." He went to the door and called.

"Angela! Angela!"

He looked keenly at the boy.

"You are not a European?"

"No, I am an American." He raised his head with a gesture of pride which became him well. "My name is Joseph Abravanel Gonzola Garrison."

The artist put his hand over his eyes: Julie's boy! The child he had held in his arms! He heard again that sweet young voice, felt the soft lips pressed against his. "I love you, Uncle Martin." Julie's boy!

Angela came in with milk, bread, and cheese. Joseph thought she was the noblest-looking woman he had ever seen.

The artist sat tracing lines on paper. He must hold that vision of the past; it would soon vanish. Angela apologized for his silence.

"My husband is sketching you, he loves beautiful heads."

Joseph sat willingly for the artist.

"It's only for myself—and for you, if you will accept it." Then pointing to a black band around the boy's arm, he said with a touch of fear, "Are you in mourning?"

"Yes, for our dearest friend, Cardinal Cabello."

"Cabello, a Cardinal? I am quite out of the world. I met him many years ago in America."

"He helped my mother bring me up. I was like his own son. I had to grieve him terribly before his death; but I couldn't help it. I must go soon again to Rome; there is a large sum of money coming to the Church from my grandmother. It was left to me conditionally—I have forfeited it."

"Don't look so sad," said the artist. "I want the brightness of you. Tell me, have you sisters and brothers."

"No, I am an only child, and very much spoilt."

"Your parents, are they—living?"

"Oh yes, and still young. My mother is the most beautiful woman in New York."

The artist caught the smile, then set him talking again, looking keenly into his face with its quick changes, its light and shade. He laughed often; he would throw back his head with a gush of merriment. That laugh thrilled the artist; it was like a far-away echo; it played on the chord of remembrance, bringing out a melody long unheard.

"You are not of pure American stock?"

"Oh yes, my mother and grandmother were born there. Mother is of Spanish-Hebrew blood. Father is of Dutch extraction; he is proud of being 'pure American'—he forgets the Indian. All others are of emigrant origin; only some came over on earlier ships. A European called us a melting pot. I hate that expression; people don't melt. We are not a smelting furnace. To me the United States is like a big Colonial mansion, with many windows made up of little panes of glass, which I call Race. Each one colors his glass with his own racial impulse."

"What color do you see?"

"Oh, my window looks toward the East where the sun rises; it is gorgeous, with many colors," laughed the boy.

"I think I catch your meaning. It would make a good symbolical picture. A great prairie, and standing in it a White House built on Colonial lines. It is flooded with a glare of strong light, which in the individual separates into its prismatic colors—the different races."

"Yes, that's what I mean; only an artist could think it out like that. Will you paint it?"

"Perhaps some day, but why not you? You have the instinct in you; I feel it."

The boy's face lit up. "How strange you should know that. I love art; I've studied it in Paris. I've been dabbling a bit in oil. They say I have talent."

The man bent forward. "I have a class of young artists in Geneva; they are all unusually gifted. Join us!" How eager he was; he hung on to the boy's answer.

"I would like it, but an artist's career is too passive for me. I have no patience. I want action, results; I want to work for the great World Reformation which is coming. I want to help bring down to this miserable, unhappy earth, a little of the Heaven we have been dreaming of so long. We must wake up! We must commence now and fight the monster of materialism which is destroying us." He was on his feet, his head erect, his eyes blazing. A young

David sharpening his sword for the great encounter with the Giant of superstition, lies, false Gods.

"I must go now. May I come again? I'm going to write all about you to my mother. Were you here that time they were caught in the storm?"

Angela put her hand on her husband's shoulder. He started, looked up.

"I was in America, I was very unfortunate there. I often lost my way—in jungles. Race instinct made me restless. The peasant blood was strong in me."

"Race instinct?" repeated the boy. "I've felt that—but I didn't know what it was, stirring in me. I can't express it. It was like a melody—from far, far away, coming back in snatches—like—like the strains of—a National Hymn. It excites me."

Angela's eyes shone.

"You are living a great romance, the romance of race."

"The romance of race, yes, that's what it is." Then he came nearer to them, and told his love story.

"Ruth is to me not only my love, she is the ideal in my life. I am going to take her out of that beautiful dark house with its old portraits. I am going to make her soul young again."

The artist went with him down the path to the bend of the road.

"Where shall I send the sketch?"

"To the College in Geneva. Would you mind if I gave it to my mother?"

"Oh, no! I will try to make it beautiful."

Joseph lingered, looking again into the artist's face with a touch of sadness.

"I feel as if I had known you a very long time."

"You have—"

He drew the boy to him and kissed him and stood watching the young figure until it disappeared.

Angela touched his arm.

"Angela! that boy! that boy!"

"Is he the son of the unhappy man who spent the night here?"

"Yes—"

The young peasant sent out a call from the barn, where he was flinging the hay lightly with a heavy pitchfork into the loft.

"What are you going to do with our boy? He does not care for books; he has no talent for painting? You are not ambitious for him—" There was a note of reproach in her voice.

"Yes, very ambitious. I want him to be what nature has made him, a peasant; nothing could be nobler."

That night the artist remained in his studio to finish the sketch; he worked for hours with intense concentration, until the pencil dropped from his numb fingers. Then he threw himself down on the couch, but couldn't rest. Ashes strewn over the fire had smothered but not extinguished it; the flames broke through. That boy! The Past living again, with all its wonder of passion, its uncontrollable love. He went to the window, leaned out; a white mist hovered over the dark valley. His eyes pierced it deeper. He was again a desperate man, holding a woman in his arms—Mad Martin!...

When the sketch was finished he painted it on ivory, framed it in silver, put it in a velvet case, and sent it to Joseph as a souvenir of their meeting. It was a speaking likeness; it went over the sea, a message to his first love.

10

The Garrisons were "at home."

The reception tonight was in honor of a distinguished Englishman. Julie stood before the mirror, putting the last touches to her toilette; she wore a creamy lace décolleté gown, with splashes of red velvet. The Gonzola diamonds glittered in her corsage.

Her maid handed her a letter and package. It was from Joseph; now the evening would be perfect.

The boy was full of hope, enthusiasm; he had just returned from Switzerland, where he saw the Val Sinestra and the old chapel she had told him about when he was a child, at night, before he went to sleep.

I visited an artist who lives near there. He's been in America; he didn't say much about himself, but he drew me out to get atmosphere for a portrait he made of me, which I am sending to you, with my best love. I am writing him a long letter; I hope he will answer. He's married to a wonderful woman; they say she has magnetic power, and it is true; she drew out all my secrets. I had to tell her about Ruth. She loves her husband with her whole soul—her eyes never leave him. They have a son, a big strong peasant lad. Mother, the artist is the most interesting man I have ever met; his hair is turning gray. He must have had a terrible struggle when he was young. I think he starved; he has deep lines in his face. I had to tear myself away. I love him, Mother, I love him! and I'm sure he loves me. When I left, he put his arms around me and kissed me; I felt his heart beating in big throbs.

"Martin's heart-beats!"

She opened the package; Joseph laughed back at her. She gazed and gazed, until the young face vanished, and she saw Martin, with her boy in his arms.

She sank down in her chair in a rush of hysterical joy.

Martin alive! Happy; no! no! not happy—content, peaceful, at work. How wonderful! Those two had met; they loved each other. God had given her absolution. How thankful she was! how thankful!

She sprang up, peered into the mirror, and saw—a white despairing face with spotted gray unkempt hair; it faded slowly; youth had touched it. A beautiful smiling woman was reflected there, with head erect, triumphant, free from that haunting fear of years.

She put out the lights and went to the door with resilient steps—then stopped, suddenly grew pale, as she looked back. The room was shadowy; one lamp shone down on the little table beside her bed, bringing out in sharp relief, the torn old Hebrew prayer book, beside it an ivory crucifix turning yellow, and—a beautiful rose, eternally young—symbols of her soul's secrets, its melody, its madness.

Finis

Milton Keynes UK
Ingram Content Group UK Ltd.
UKHW030741071024
449371UK00006B/671

9 789362 921383